PROFESSIONAL ENGLISH - II

AS PER THE ANNA UNIVERSITY LATEST SYLLABUS FOR SECOND SEMESTER B.E / B.TECH STUDENTS

SHARMILA MANGALARAJA

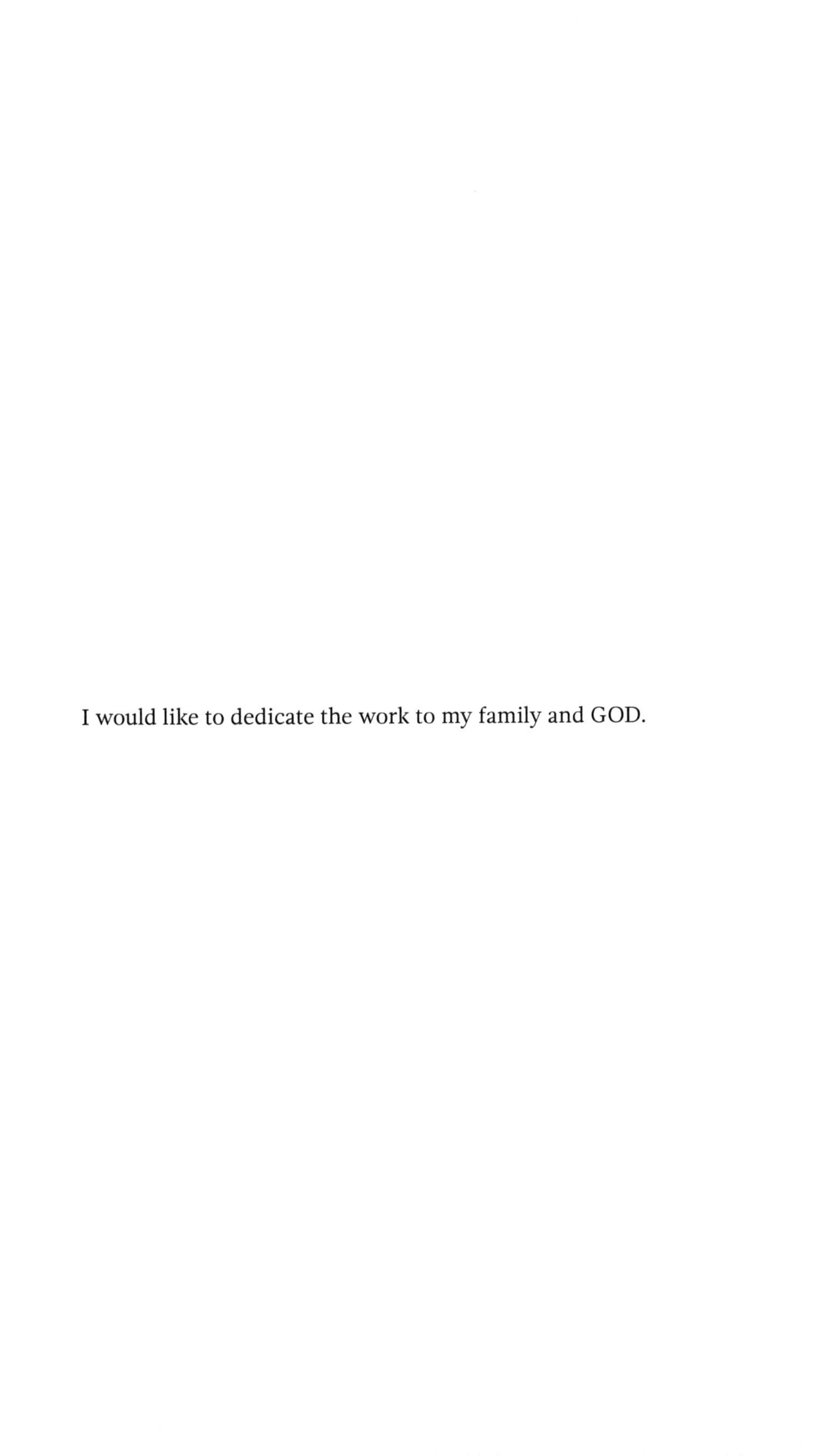

I would like to dedicate the work to my family and GOD.

Contents

Contents

Foreword

Mrs.Sharmila Mangalaraja's long tenure in the field of teaching allows her to provide guidance and direction for the youngsters. She graduated from M.K. University and holds Master of Philosophy in English Literature. She has successfully presented 11 papers including International level. And she has worked in both India as well as Dubai. Her vision and knowledge has led her to many successful. All her success in whole heartedly dedicated to her family. Though her resources, she is enthusiastic about educating others.

Preface

Communication is an imperative aspect of life. Communication skills are fundamental in all circles of life. The victory of a try pivots on the capacity to communicate viably in today's quick paced life. In such a situation viable communication holds the key. Communication could be a key instrument to make and fortify relations between two individuals or a bunch of individuals. Without communication strategies, there are no human relations

This book Professional Communication Text Book – II outlined in a comprehensive way and will be accommodating for the building engineers to create their four fundamental abilities of communication – Listening, Speaking, Reading and Writing (perusing, talking, tuning in and composing).

This book is outlined with specialized points which can offer assistance the understudies to create their lexicon, language structure, articulation and other essential aptitudes that are exceptionally much required for successful communication.

We are obligated to **Notion Press** distributers for their fast, expedient and quality distribution. Suggestions, valuable feedback for encourage enhancement of the book will be exceedingly recognized.

-Mrs.Sharmila Mangalaraja M.Phil.,

Acknowledgements

SYLLABUS

HS3251 PROFESSIONAL ENGLISH - II L T P C

3 1 0 4

COURSE OBJECTIVES:

- To engage learners in meaningful language activities to improve their LSRW skills
- To enhance learners' awareness of general rules of writing for specific audiences
- To help learners understand the purpose, audience, contexts of different types of writing
- To develop analytical thinking skills for problem solving in communicative contexts
- To demonstrate an understanding of job applications and interviews for internship and placements

UNIT I: MAKING COMPARISONS 12

Listening – Evaluative Listening: Advertisements, Product Descriptions, -Audio / video; Listening and filling a Graphic Organiser (Choosing a product or service by comparison) **Speaking** – Marketing a product, Persuasive Speech Techniques. **Reading** - Reading advertisements, user manuals, brochures; **Writing** – Professional emails, Email etiquette - Compare and Contrast Essay; **Grammar** – Mixed Tenses, Prepositional phrases **Vocabulary** – Contextual meaning of words.

UNIT II: EXPRESSING CAUSAL RELATIONS IN SPEAKING AND WRITING 12

Listening - Listening to longer technical talks and completing– gap filling exercises. Listening technical information from podcasts – Listening to process/event descriptions to identify cause & effects - **Speaking** – Describing and discussing the reasons of accidents or disasters based on news reports. **Reading** - Reading longer technical texts– Cause and Effect Essays, and Letters / emails of complaint, **Writing** - Writing responses to complaints. **Grammar** - Active Passive Voice transformations, Infinitive and

Gerunds **Vocabulary** – Word Formation (Noun-Verb-Adj-Adv), Adverbs.

UNIT III: PROBLEM SOLVING 12

Listening – Listening to / Watching movie scenes/ documentaries depicting a technical problem and suggesting solutions. **Speaking** – Group Discussion(based on case studies), - techniques and Strategies, **Reading** - Case Studies, excerpts from literary texts, news reports etc., **Writing** – Letter to the Editor, Checklists, Problem solution essay / Argumentative Essay **Grammar** – Error correction; If conditional sentences **Vocabulary** - Compound Words, Sentence Completion.

UNIT IV: REPORTING OF EVENTS AND RESEARCH 12

Listening – Listening Comprehension based on news reports – and documentaries – Precis writing, Summarising, **Speaking** –Interviewing, Presenting an oral report, Mini presentations on select topics; **Reading** –Newspaper articles; **Writing** – Recommendations, Transcoding, Accident Report, Survey Report **Grammar** – Reported Speech, Modals **Vocabulary** – Conjunctions- use of prepositions.

UNIT V: THE ABILITY TO PUT IDEAS OR INFORMATION COGENTLY 12

Listening – Listening to TED Talks, Presentations, Formal job interviews, (analysis of the interview performance); **Speaking** – Participating in a Role play, (interview/telephone interview), virtual interviews, Making presentations with visual aids; **Reading** – Company profiles, Statement of Purpose, (SOP), an excerpt of interview with professionals; **Writing** – Job / Internship application – Cover letter & Resume; **Grammar** – Numerical adjectives, Relative Clauses **Vocabulary** – Idioms.

COURSE OUTCOMES:

At the end of the course, learners will be able

- To compare and contrast products and ideas in technical texts.
- To identify cause and effects in events, industrial processes through technical texts
- To analyze problems in order to arrive at feasible solutions and communicate them orally and in the written format.
- To report events and the processes of technical and industrial nature.
- To present their opinions in a planned and logical manner, and draft effective resumes in context of job search.

TEXT BOOKS:

1. English for Engineers & Technologists (2020 edition) Orient Blackswan Private Ltd. Department of English, Anna University.

2. English for Science & Technology Cambridge University Press 2021.Dr. Veena Selvam, Dr. Sujatha Priyadarshini, Dr. Deepa Mary Francis, Dr. KN. Shoba, and Dr. Lourdes Joevani, Department of English, Anna University.

REFERENCES:

1. Raman. Meenakshi, Sharma. Sangeeta (2019). Professional English. Oxford university press. New Delhi.

2. Improve Your Writing ed. V.N. Arora and Laxmi Chandra, Oxford Univ. Press, 2001, New Delhi.

3. Learning to Communicate – Dr. V. Chellammal. Allied Publishers, New Delhi, 2003

4. Business Correspondence and Report Writing by Prof. R.C. Sharma & Krishna Mohan, Tata McGraw Hill & Co. Ltd., 2001, New Delhi.

5. Krishna Mohan, Meera Banerji, "Developing Communication Skills", Trinity Press, 2017.

CHAPTER ONE

UNIT I: MAKING COMPARISONS PROFESSIONAL EMAILS

E-mail (Electronic Postal) was one of the most important inventions in the early 1960s, revolutionizing mail systems. Emailing and messaging became possible with the introduction of time-sharing computers. Previously, communications were sent through a physical medium such as paper and postal services. With the introduction of E-mail, which allows people to communicate messages to one another via computers, a breakthrough was accomplished. If a person has access to a computer with an adequate internet connection, he or she can send or read messages from anywhere in the world. Sending e-mails is a convenient way for people to communicate with one another. With today's mobile phones, everyone may send, receive, and check E-mails at any time.

Advantages of E-mail:

- Cheap and quick
- Short and informative
- Send and receive messages in a matter of seconds regardless of time and place
- Scheduled and sent at anytime across the globe despite of different global time zones.
- Sent to either one or a group at a same time

E-mail disadvantages

- possibility of receiving junk mail,
- A lack of privacy and security.

- Most recent update - encryption capability - allows users to share content in a safe and secure manner.

Professional E-mails

These are the email addresses that are used for professional and commercial correspondence. It has a different tone and format than personal/informal emails. The following six stages must be considered while writing a well-written professional e-mail.

- Identify the purpose,
- Target the audience,
- Keep everything in sync.
- Proofread your correspondence
- Follow basic etiquette.

How to write a Professional email?

Consider the goal and sketch up a basic layout. This serves as a guideline for understanding the letter's objective.

1. Make use of a professional typeface. Instead, choose conservative typefaces like Times New Roman and Arial. Avoid using ornamental fonts such as Comic Sans or Old English. The best font size for reading is 12point type. Use plain typefaces instead than fancy ones like Comic Sans or Old English. It's best to avoid using all capitals since it may come out as yelling at the receiver.
2. Make a topic that is appropriate. This is a sneak peek of what's to come. Keep it succinct and under 60 characters. Emphasize the goal and be as detailed as possible. Subjects like "schedule," "Guest List," "Lunch Request," "Meeting over view of (date)," "Contacting you," and "Email regarding an essential problem" are overly broad, too lengthy, or include many topics. "Meeting RE: broken escalator on March 12th," for example, is a brief subject that indicates the main issue and a specific date.
3. Begin with a warm welcome. "Respected Sir/ Madam," "Dear Mr./Ms./Mrs./Dr. ________(preferably the last name)," "Dear Mr./Ms./Mrs./Dr. ________(preferably the last name)," "Dear Mr./Ms./Mrs./Dr. ________(preferably the last name)," "Dear Mr./Ms./

"To Whom It May Concern" is a phrase that means "to whom it may concern" (if the recipient is unknown). This shall be followed by other phrases of greetings such as "Warm Greetings!", "Greating to you!", "Good morning/noon/evening." "Hello" and such casual salutations should be avoided.

4. **Compose an opening statement.**

Introduction. Give a brief overview of yourself. This can be a one- or two-line paragraph. The sender's name can be connected to Linkedin profiles, allowing the receiver to learn more about the sender. Keep things simple.

Thank the recipient

Please express gratitude to the receiver. If the email is a response to a previous email or client query, it should begin with a line of appreciation, such as "Thank you for contacting us," "I appreciate you," "I am thankful for your efforts on my behalf," or "Thank you for cooperating."

1. **Declare the goal** Include a clear description of what you're trying to say, as well as how the receiver will benefit and what they should do next. Keep the email's body to a minimum. Make the e-mail as skimmable as possible. Jargon should be avoided. If the content and purpose of the email merit them, use bold, italics, and highlights.
2. **End with an appropriate closing.** Conclude the email with proper sign-off such as "Have a good day", "Regards", "Best", "Best regards", "Thanks", "Sincerely", "Kind regards"
3. **Include an e-mail signature**. This has the potential to share information about the job and company. This includes name, role, company name and website, hyperlinked contacts.
4. **Add your closing remarks.** Ask an open ended question to increase the chances of getting a reply. This is optional.

E-mail Etiquette

E-mail etiquette is a set of rules for sending and receiving emails. Email etiquette has its dos and don'ts.

Do's and Don'ts

- Make sure your topic line is clear.
- Make use of a formal salute and formal language.
- Use slang, emotions, vulgarity, jokes, and humour sparingly.
- Do prefer active voice
- Don't forget to include your email signature.
- Make use of professional email address

Professional E-mail address

It should not be a username or a nickname, but rather a variant of the user's true name. To secure an e-mail address, use periods, hyphens, or underscores.

Avoid using numerals and other letters if at all feasible.

Eg: sharmila.raja@gmail.com

Examples:

1.Shri Raj Electronics recently sold you an ABC colour TV. The kit has issues and is defective. To seek replacement of the kit, send an email to the Sales and Service Manager.

To: sharmilaraja@gmail.com

CC:suthosia1990@gmail.com

BCC:rajesh1990@gmail.com

Subject: a malfunctioning television set

On April 25, 2022 (previous date), I acquired a new 34-inch LCD color television set from your shop. SRE/2052/2022 is the bill number assigned to it. At my place, you installed the set. However, only two days after installation, the set began to malfunction and cause several issues. Initially, it was only the sound that was failing, but as time went on, the picture became wavy as well.

Despite your customer service department's repeated claims, no one has shown up to repair or replace the broken television. Trying to contact your customer service department while watching a broken television has become a nuisance. The situation has not changed as a result of my many reminders. I hope you will see the situation and replace the set as soon as possible to maintain the image of your company.

Regards

Seema

Exercises:

1. Send an e-mail to your Principal seeking permission to participate in a project in Delhi.

2. Send an e-mail to a manager requesting permission to visit the company.

3. Assume you are a third year student representative. Send an e-mail to your college's chairman, suggesting that he award merit scholarships to the students.

4. Send an email to the course coordinator, Fun Activities Pvt.Ltd, Rishikesh, and ask for details of all the adventure activities they offer during the summer holidays.

5. Email your high school science teacher and ask him or her to help you with a science project you need to do over summer break. You are Siva from Chandigarh.

Compare and contrast Essay

A compare-and-contrast essay is a type of essay that compares and contrasts two or more subjects. It's perfect for demonstrating what distinguishes and connects similar items or concepts, especially when the subjects are frequently misunderstood for one another or unfairly grouped together.

Compare-and-contrast essays have a lot in common with other sorts of essays, but they also differ in a number of ways—which is the whole point of comparing and contrasting! The reader gains a better understanding of each subject by utilizing the other as a frame of reference by observing the contrasts and similarities.

Purpose of the Essay:

Let's imagine you're writing an article about how wonderful renewable resources are, but you spend a lot of time discussing how fossil fuels operate. Your reader needs a little history on their alternative, fossil fuels, to really appreciate why renewable resources are so amazing—but the essay's focus is divided so evenly that it feels like there are two topics.

That is when compare-and-contrast essays are at their most effective. If two issues are related or define each other, highlighting their similarities and distinctions can help you better describe them both. This is especially true for topics that are frequently conflated or confused for one another; it aids readers when someone points out what is similar and what is different about them.

Unlike argumentative or persuasive essays, comparison-and-contrast essays compare and contrast several subjects rather than focusing on just one. The disadvantage is that they do not provide as much detail about particular themes as single-topic essays. They're also a typical college essay assignment since they demonstrate to the instructor how well you understand both disciplines.

How to write a compare-and-contrast essay

After you've decided on your topics, you may start brainstorming ideas. It's a good idea to start by making a list of all the similarities and contrasts between your subjects. You may start making connections and deciding on a framework for your compare-and-contrast essay once you have them all written down.

Compare and Contrast Venn Diagram

Make a Venn diagram if you get stuck. This is a diagram that shows you the traits your subjects have in common and which ones they don't.

Organization:

The format of compare-and-contrast essays is based on our own recommendations. While the linked guide goes into further detail, in a nutshell, your compare-and-contrast essay should have the following structure:

- **Introduction**: Where you explain your thesis or what your essay will discuss
- **Body**: where you actually list the similarities and differences of your subjects; the largest section

Conclusion: where you wrap up and summarize your points

Examples:

1. "High School vs. College"

Many individuals feel that college is simply an extension of high school. When you go into a college campus, however, you can't deny the disparities between the two. It's not just about the newfound freedom. Examine the organisation, teaching style, and grading to see how college and high school are similar and different. The framework is obvious in high school. The majority of kids have been following it for at least the last eight years leading up to high school graduation. Students learn diverse disciplines in regular time increments for roughly 6 hours per day or 30 hours per week.

Additionally, professors provide lectures using textbooks and chalkboard notes. During lectures, students ask questions and take notes. The majority of the time, the lecture is based on the textbook. Furthermore, high school students receive grades depending on how well they understand the topic, using state textbooks and established rubrics. Teachers assess students' abilities through assignments, tests, and quizzes. Additionally, pupils are given supplemental or extra credit in order to help them improve their grades.

While there is structure in college, it is not the same as in high school. Students adhere to a timetable, but it is one that they set for themselves. Full-time college students spend 12 to 18 hours per week in class, rather than 6 hours per day. The school year is divided into four semesters or quarters: fall, winter, spring, and summer.

Furthermore, college professors do not follow the book when it comes to teaching approaches. While books can help with learning, their lectures are jam-packed with interactive materials, visuals, personal experience, and subject knowledge. Teachers expect students to gather material on their own through research projects and homework rather than being given all of it. It is also the obligation of pupils to seek out teachers if they have any questions.

Finally, professors expect students to apply what they've learned, therefore marking is based more on a student's ability to apply what they've learned to specific situations. Tests can also make or break a student's grade. Some lecturers only test this information a couple times during the semester. If you fail a test, you may fail the course. Both high school and college are higher education institutions that use class and grading frameworks. But that's where the resemblances end. These two colleges have entirely distinct structures, instructional methodologies, and grading ways.

KEY TAKE AWAYS

- A compare-and-contrast essay analyzes two subjects by either comparing them, contrasting them, or both.
- The purpose of writing a comparison or contrast essay is not to state the obvious but rather to illuminate subtle differences or unexpected similarities between two subjects.
- The thesis should clearly state the subjects that are to be compared, contrasted, or both, and it should state what is to be learned from doing so.
- There are two main organizing strategies for compare-and-contrast essays.
- Organize by the subjects themselves, one then the other.
- Organize by individual points, in which you discuss each subject in relation to each point.
- Use phrases of comparison or phrases of contrast to signal to readers how exactly the two subjects are being analyzed.

EXERCISES:

Compare and Contrast the Following Questions:

1. 3D movies or 4D movies
2. Virtual Vs real classrooms
3. Higher education or job
4. 3G Vs 4G
5. Joint Family Vs Nuclear Family

MIXED TENSES

We look at commonly confusing words like "its" vs. "it's" in our regular Grammar class. We'll look at verb tenses this time. When employed wrongly, verb tenses can cause a lot of confusion about how an action relates to time. We recommend that you become familiar with the various verb tenses, as verbs can take on different forms depending on the tenses in which they are used. To grasp tenses, however, you only need to know the logic and recall a few phrase forms and general guidelines. It will become second nature to you after some practise. Let's get this party started.

Here is a list or rules of these tenses

	Simple Forms	Progressive Forms	Perfect Forms	Perfect Progressive Forms
Present	Ist form + s / es	am/is/are + Ist form + ing	have/has + IIIrd form	have/has been + Ist form + ing
Past	IInd form	was/were + Ist form + ing	had + IIIrd form	had been + Ist form + ing
Future	will/shall + Ist form	will be + Ist form + ing	will have + IIIrd form	will have been + Ist form + ing

Rules

Present Tense

Present Simple

The present tense is used to refer to events, actions, and conditions that occur frequently or exist right now.

- "I sleep every day."
- "She plays football."

Present Continuous:

The present tense is used for acts that are taking place right now or for actions that are not yet completed. When the action is transient, this tense is also utilized.

- "I am swimming in my neighbor's pool now."
- "He is speaking to my mum at the moment."

Present Perfect:

The tense that is used for something that started in the past and continued to the present time.

- "I have swum in the sea countless times."
- "I have spoken to her many times."

Present Perfect Continuous:

The present tense is used to express that something began in the past and is still happening now.

- "I have been singing since I was 9 years old."
- "She has been competing in dance competitions lately."

Past Tense

Simple Past:

The past tense is used to describe an event or action that occurred previously.

- "Yesterday, I swam 10 laps."
- "Last night, I cooked mutton gravy."

Past Continuous:

The present tense is used to describe a continuous action or occurrence that began or occurred in the past. It can also be used to indicate a task that was left undone due to another event or action.

- "I was swimming with my friend last night when Boby arrived."
- "In March, she was teaching in a school in Chennai."

Past Perfect:

The tense that is used to make it clear that one event happened before another in the past.

- "I had swum the breaststroke before I turned 8."
- "He had failed to communicate that he had another wife when we first met."

Past Perfect Continuous:

The tense used to express that an action began in the past and continued until a later point in time.

- "I had been swimming for many years before priya picked up the sport."
- "Dave had been playing soccer for 10 years when he was offered a spot on the US Olympic team."

Future Tense

Simple Future:

The present tense is used to describe events that have not yet occurred but are expected or likely to occur in the future.

- "I will swim more than 12 laps tomorrow."
- "You will see her again next week."

Future Continuous:

The future tense is used to describe an unfinished action or event that will take place in the future and continue for an estimated amount of time.

- "I will be swimming in the new Olympic-sized swimming pool on Friday."
- "By December next year, I will be swimming like a fish."

Future Perfect:

The tense that is used for actions that will be completed between now and some point in the future.

- "I will have swum at least 1000km by the end of the year"
- "He will have built 40 homes by the first quarter of 2018."

Future Perfect Continuous:

The present tense is used to indicate acts that will continue until a future point.

- "By noon today, I will have been swimming for 2 hours."
- "In April, Damien will have been working in the company for 10 years."

Exercises:

1. When I opened the door, my friend______(enter).

2. Every morning she_____(wake) up early and gets ready for work.
3. If I knew what he ___(want), I would not permit this.
4. I ________(heard) anything from her in a long time.
5. The headmaster _____(want) to talk to you.
6. Jane _______(live) with her parents.
7. We _______(visit) Greece next month.
8. The moon ______(revolve) around the earth.
9. She _______(write) a novel.
10. All students _____ (hand) in their work.

Answers:

1. **Entered**
2. **Wakes**
3. **Wanted**
4. **Haven't heard**
5. **Wants**
6. **Lives**
7. **Are visiting**
8. **Revolves**
9. **Has written**
10. **Have handed**

Prepositional phrases

A prepositional phrase is a collection of words that includes a preposition, its object, and any modifiers to the object. A prepositional phrase almost often modifies a verb or a noun. Adverbial phrases and adjectival phrases are two types of prepositional phrases.

A prepositional phrase must have at least one preposition and the object it governs. A noun, a gerund (a verb form ending in "-ing" that serves as a noun), or a clause can be used as the object.

Prepositional phrases that modify nouns:

When a prepositional phrase acts upon a noun, we say it is behaving adjectivally because adjectives modify nouns. A prepositional phrase that behaves adjectivally is called, quite logically, an adjectival phrase.

Example: The dog in the middle is the cutest.

Prepositional phrases that modify verbs:

Because adverbs modify verbs, we say a prepositional phrase is acting adverbially when it operates on a verb. Adverbial phrases are prepositional phrases that behave adverbially.

Example: To find the person who stole the last cookie,
look behind you.

List of Prepositions

About	below	from	through	along
behind	for	past	against	beyond
Except	over	after	between	into
outside	across	beside	inside	under
Above	beneath	in	to	among

List of Prepositions

Examples:

Along with, on behalf of, because of, inspite of, in front of, in accordance with, in order to, in the event of, by means of, for the sake of, with reference to, on according to, Down the tree, Up the hill, Around the mulberry bush, Into the woods, With chopped nuts, Near a fast-flowing river, Within the book's pages, Through the tunnel

Exercise:

1. There are lots of birds nesting ______________

2. Before school, the boys played tag _________

3. Come ________with me.

4. ___________the chair sat moldering in the attic.

5. I gave the children pizza _______pancakes for breakfast today.

6. She caught the bus_________.

7. That girl __________is so happy.

8. I like to go grocery shopping at the department stores______________.

9. Sheela cheered for her team_______.

10. The boy ________________is the best player.

Answers:

1. under the leaves.

2. at the park.

3. into the store

4. for one hundred years

5. instead of

6. on time

7. at the park

8. behind my house

9. with excitement

10. in the middle

Contextual meaning of words

There are multiple meanings to certain words and phrases. The meaning of a word alters or differs depending on its context in the sentence. Context clues are hints; a reader can use to discover the meanings of unfamiliar words and phrases.

Contextual Meaning

Example 1:

1.Education is a fundamental right

2.Turn right

3.She is all right

4.You are right

The word 'right' in the first line refers to something that one is ethically or legally entitled to. The word 'right' in the second sentence denotes a movement to the right. In the third statement, 'right' denotes that the individual is fine, whereas in the fourth sentence, 'right' denotes that the person is correct.

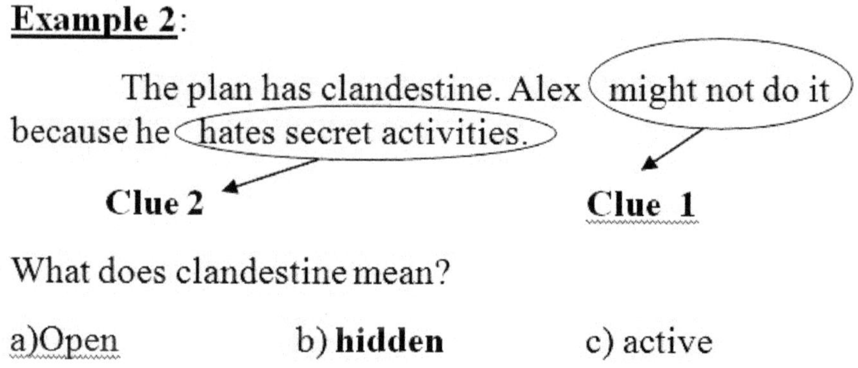

Example 3

Indentify the contextual meaning of the underlined word

a)The children crowded around the teacher. – (Ans.Gather)

b) He was backed up by his team to fight for his rights. – (Ans: To support, to sustain)

Example 4

Fill in the blanks with the contextual meaning

a) There was nobody ____________ at the railway station – (Ans: to see her off)

Example 5

Write the correct meaning of the given proverb

a) Every dog has its day – (Ans: Every person will have success or good fortune sometime)

Example 6

Fill in the blanks with the contextual meaning

a)She was afraid as they were ________of time to submit their projects(Ans: running out)

Example 7:

She thinks the house is valuable, but this is incorrect. The house is worthless.

1.What does worthless mean?

a.inaccurate b. **not valuable** c. Strange

Different forms of clues are used by authors:

- **Examples** – The restaurant **ambiance** including its quiet music, flowers and candle light made it a perfect pace for party.

In this sentence they used examples such as music, flowers. By reading the text we can understand the meaning of ambiance. i.e.atmosphere or mood

- **Synonyms** – The child's ability to perform gymnastics are **apparent or obvious** at an early age.

In this sentence, if you look at the word apparent, Obvious is the synonyms of apparent and easy to understand.

- **Antonyms** – Sheela was **meticulous** with her assignments like her brother, Ravi , who scribbled all over the page

In this sentence, if you don't know the meaning of the word meticulous means look at the word scribbled. Then we can understand that meticulous means **neat and careful.**

- **Definitions** – Ashok was repulsed by the spider crawling up her arm. She had a feeling of disgust and dislike.

In the above sentence, we learn the meaning of repelled by reading a feeling of disgust and dislike, which is the definition.

Exercises:

Indentify the contextual meaning of the underlined word

1.It was the time for the band to march on the field. The crowd was **<u>ecstatic</u>**! People screamed and cheered showing their excitement. The music is **<u>intensified</u>** or increased in volume. Unlike her **<u>timid</u>** friends, ramesh was unafraid to perform in front of the roaring crowd. After the show, the crowd gave a standing **<u>ovation</u>**. The fans stood and clapped to show their appreciation for such a great performance.

(Ans: Excited, Increased, afraid or shy, applause or clapping)

KEY TAKE AWAYS

- Look for context clues that restate ideas or opposite situations.
- Use prior knowledge about the content of the text or the meaning of the word.
- Look for signal words

CHAPTER TWO

UNIT II: EXPRESSING CAUSAL RELATIONS IN SPEAKING AND WRITING WRITING RESPONSES TO COMPLAINTS

Writing an effective response to a customer complaint can help you keep valuable consumers while also reinforcing your company's favorable brand image. In this lesson, we'll go through how to write a meaningful customer complaint response, as well as some writing ideas and a sample response that you can use as a model.

Guides

i. Use a kind, empathetic tone.
v. Don't squabble.
v. Even if you disagree with the complaint and have no way of resolving it, a thoughtful response can frequently help calm an enraged customer.

Why Customer Complaints Are Retention Gold?

Customer retention should be a primary concern for any company seeking long-term success.

v. Return clients are worth up to ten times what they paid the first time.

v. Getting a new client is seven times more expensive than keeping an existing one.

• Selling to existing clients is six times easier than selling to new consumers.

• Increase client retention

• Reinforce your brand's favorable image

• Reduce negative word-of-mouth about your service or product

• Positive word-of-mouth about your customer service will increase.

So, if our goal is to keep customers, why are complaints so important? In short, client complaints are a rich mine of information that helps us better understand our customer base and retain them.

Twenty-six customers remain silent for everyone who complains. In other words, complaints provide us with information about potentially widespread issues that are affecting a substantial portion of our consumer base. When they criticize, customers are actively teaching you how to enhance your product.

Furthermore, when you effectively handle a client complaint, their likelihood of doing business with you again increases. If they had never complained in the first place, "Successfully resolve" is the essential phrase here, and that's what we'll talk about in the next part.

How to write a strong customer complaint response?

When responding to a customer complaint, consider the following steps:

1**. Read the entire complaint:**

Read the entire complaint thoroughly before composing your response. As a way of confirming the customer's frustration, make sure you grasp the specifics of the incident in question. And then reiterate those details in your response.

2. **Apologize for any inconvenience:**

Beginning your response with an apology if there was a misunderstanding and the company has not made an error, you can still apologize for any inconvenience or confusion that has arisen.

3. **Explain what may have caused the issue:**

Customers may be more satisfied if they understand why they were inconvenienced by the situation. Consider and discuss the process behind why the consumer experienced this inconvenience in as much detail as feasible.

4. <u>Propose an actionable, detailed solution:</u>

The action that the corporation proposes to take as compensation for the client is one of the most significant components of the customer complaint response letter. This can encompass a variety of things, including:

- A product replacement offer
- Service rescheduling
- The product or service will be refunded.

5. <u>Explain how you can improve the customer's experience in the future:</u>

After confirming that your organization will remedy the situation, the following step should be to outline how your company intends to improve the customer's experience in the future. The more information you can provide about the future of better customer service, the more valuable your comment will appear.

<u>6. Offer an incentive:</u>

If possible, offer an incentive to your customer in your response letter. This can be anything from a discount for a product subscription to an upgrade to a better version of a product.

<u>7. Encourage customer response</u>

Encourage the consumer to react with any additional questions or issues they may have regarding your product or service at the end of your letter. Being open to conversation demonstrates to your customer that you care about keeping them as a customer.

<u>8. Reply to any follow-up letters or questions</u>

Respond to any additional letters from your consumer. Responding quickly and honestly shows your customers that you value their business.

Tips for responding to customer complaints

Consider the following suggestions while creating your customer complaint response letter:

v. **Address the customer by name**

Make sure your customer's name is included, and double-check that you have spelled it correctly. You will appear more empathetic and personal if you avoid using a generic greeting and instead address your customer directly.

v. **Consider the customer's point of view**

When writing your response, think about the customer's point of view. How would you react if something similar happened to you? How would you like your complaint to be handled by a company? Considering the customer's perspective can assist you in crafting an empathic answer.

v. **Respond as promptly as possible**

A prompt answer demonstrates to the customer that you value their feedback and loyalty. Take your time to fully comprehend the concern, but respond as quickly as possible.

Example 1:

Here is an example of a response to a typical customer complaint:

Dear John

Your complaint about the damaged item you received as part of your recent online order has been received. We're sorry this happened, and we understand how inconvenient it has been for you. We have already sent you a replacement item at no cost, which you should receive within two business days.

We appreciate your dedication as a client and would like to offer you a ten percent discount on your next purchase. Please let us know if there is anything else we can do to make you're buying experience with us more pleasant, and we appreciate your comments.

Sincerely,

Acme Craft Supplies.

Example 2:

Here's their response, which you can use as a template for your clients:

Dear Rajesh,

Please accept my heartfelt apologies for any inconvenience these problems have caused you. I've gone ahead and resubmitted any of your listings that were wrongly rejected by Broken Site. Your listings that were refused for blocked sites were also declined for duplication of results, according to my research. This means that the keywords you were trying to add to your account were already there and were considered a duplicate of an existing listing. This indicates that the terms you wanted to add are already in your account.

Following additional analysis, it was determined that your site does not provide a product or service with which Yahoo! is not associated, and thus the blocked site decline reason was erroneous. This reason for rejection has no bearing on the outcome of your submission.

The keywords that were rejected due to a lack of content were rejected correctly. You tried bidding on keywords like "business coach executive professional" and "life and business coach," but it's unclear whether a customer can discover a business coach on your site or if they'll be referred to a third party for help. You might be authorized for such keywords if you provide more information in the "Find an Executive Coach" section of your website.

You might be pleased to learn that Yahoo! is working on a new advertiser interface that will provide businesses with a more powerful advertising experience, and we hope to launch it in the second half of this year.

I understand that you would like to adjust a few items in your account, and I just wanted to let you know that we value advertising input and are constantly seeking to enhance our services. We'd love to hear from you if you have any more suggestions.

Please do not hesitate to contact us if we can be of any further assistance. Thank you for choosing Yahoo!

Sincerely,

G.S.Yuththika [NAME]

Executive Services

Yahoo! Search Marketing

Example 3:

Acknowledging Receipt of a Customer complaint

When a customer submits a complaint through any communication channel, it's important to let them know that their voice was heard and that the relevant company contacts have been notified.

Dear [Name],

I'm sorry to hear you were on hold for 30 minutes with our customer support department. I can imagine how aggravating this has been for you. This should not have happened because we appreciate our clients' time.

This message will be forwarded to the proper department and customer support agent. We've prioritized the problem you're having with our product, and our team is already hard at work to fix it. I'll let you know as soon as it's corrected.

I appreciate you sharing your unpleasant experience with us. I apologize for the trouble this has caused. We try to deliver outstanding customer service in a timely manner. Please contact us if you have any further questions, complaints, or suggestions.

Warm Regards,

Timonika.P (Your Name)

Customer Service Director

(As this example demonstrates, the optimal response is one that is individualized and respects the precise issues stated by the consumer. They've also included the statement, "Our staff is already actively working to remedy the issue." I'll let you know as soon as it's corrected." This assurance informs the customer that a follow-up email will be issued directly from the representative who sent the initial email response.)

Example 4:

Responding to Dissatisfaction with Overall Customer Experience

There will be moments when a consumer is unsatisfied yet unable to articulate their dissatisfaction. It could be because they ran into many problems or simply had a bad customer service experience. In any case, your customer service department may receive a complaint expressing general displeasure. In this scenario, acknowledging the customer's discontent and expressing your wish to assist them in clarifying their issue is the best course of action.

Dear [Name],

Thank you for your email. We take customer satisfaction seriously and are glad to hear from you.

First and foremost, I apologize for the recent frustration you've been experiencing. I'd want to express our gratitude for your input. It will enable us to address any issues that arise and enhance our services.

We're honored that you've chosen us as your service provider for the past five years, and we'd appreciate the chance to address your issues and earn your continuing trust.

We'd appreciate it if you could fill out the accompanying form with further details about your experience to assist us route your complaint to the proper department that can handle your issues.

We apologize for any inconvenience this has caused you, and we aim to provide you with better services in the future.

Best regards,

G.S.Shivanesh Kumar

Customer Service Director

Example 5:

Handling a Delivery Delay

With the increased competition for expedited shipping services, providing clients with a credible estimate for their goods delivery has become a must. A product that does not arrive on time is one of the most common – and frustrating – situations that customers may encounter. Delayed deliveries can be a difficult problem for your service staff to deal with because they must work in tandem with your delivery service provider.

When a product delivery is delayed, a note with a helpful tone is excellent.

Greetings, [Name],

I am so disappointed to learn that your order has not yet arrived. I can imagine how aggravating this is.

I've checked the status of your shipment with the US Postal Service, and it's presently [status]. If you'd want to keep track of the status of your shipment, go to this link: [link]

If your package has not arrived by [date], please answer to this message and let me know. You can also contact me directly at 1-234-567-8910.

Please accept my heartfelt apologies for any inconvenience this has caused.

Best,

Jack

Customer Service Representative

Exercises:

1.Write a letter to respond to a complaint on a Manager's attitude.

2. Write a letter to respond to a complaint on a website error

3. Write a letter to respond to a complaint on the customer's dissatisfaction.

Active Passive Voice transformations

In English grammar, verbs have five properties: voice, mood, tense, person, and number; here, we are concerned with voice. The two grammatical voices are active and passive.

What's the difference between active and passive voice?

Active Voice

The active voice is used when the sentence's subject executes the verb's action. The active voice uses a forceful, direct, and distinct tone in their sentences. Here are a few instances of active voice that are brief and simple.

Active voice examples

i. Monkeys adore bananas.
v. The cashier counted the money.
v. The dog chased the squirrel.

All three sentences have a basic active voice construction: subject, verb, and object. The subject monkey performs the action described by adore. The subject the cashier performs the action described by counted. The subject the dog performs the action described by chased. The subjects are doing, doing, doing—they take action in their sentences. The active voice reminds us of the popular like slogan, "Just Do It."

Passive voice

When the verb acts on the subject, the sentence is said to be in the passive voice. The passive voice is always made up of a conjugated form of to be and the past participle of the verb. This frequently results in the formation of a preposition. That sounds a lot harder than it is—passive voice is really easy to spot. To demonstrate the distinction between active and passive voice, we will change the three active statements above.

Passive voice examples

v. Bananas are adored by monkeys.
v. The money was counted by the cashier.
v. The squirrel was chased by the dog.

Let's take a closer look at the first pair of sentences, "Monkeys adore bananas" and "Bananas are adored by monkeys." The active sentence consists of monkeys (subject) + adore (verb) + bananas (object). The passive sentence consists of bananas (object) + are adored (a form of to be plus the past participle adored) + by (preposition) + monkeys (subject). Making the sentence passive flipped the structure and necessitated the preposition by. In fact, all three of the transformed sentences above required the addition of by.

When to use active and passive voice

The active voice has a stronger, clearer tone than the passive voice, which is more subtle and weak. Here's some sensible advice: don't use the passive voice simply because it sounds more elegant than the active voice.

That said there are times the passive voice is useful and called for. Take "The squirrel was chased by the dog," for example. That sentence construction would be helpful if the squirrel were the focus of your writing and not the dog.

Passive voice is used sometimes due to the following reasons.

1. When intentionally hiding the subject of sentence.
2. When passive voice better explain thought of sentence.
3. When passive voice better emphasizes the main though of the sentence.
4. When subject is not exactly known.

Fundamental Rules for changing from active voice to passive voice

1. The places of subject and object are interchanged i.e. the object shifts to the place of subject and subject shifts to the place of object in passive voice.

Example.

Active voice : I write a letter.

Passive voice : A letter is written by me.

Subject (I) of sentence shifted to the place of object (letter) and object (letter) shifted to the place of subject (I) in passive voice.

2. Sometimes subject of sentence is not used in passive voice. Subject of sentence can be omitted in passive voice, if without subject it can give enough meaning in passive voice.

Example

Passive voice: cloth is sold in yards

3. 3rd form of verb (past participle) is always used as main verb in sentences of passive voice for all tenses. Base form of verb or present participle will be never used in passive voice.

The word "by" is used before subject in sentences in passive voice.

Example.

Active voice : He sings a song.

Passive voice : A song is sung **by** him.

4. The word "by" is not always used before subject in passive voice. Sometimes words "with, to, etc" may also be used before subject in passive voice.

Examples.

Active voice: The water fills the tub.

Passive voice: The tub is filled **with** water.

Active voice: He knows me.

Passive voice: I am known **to** him.

5. Auxiliary verbs are used passive voice according to the tense of sentence

- The places of subject and object in sentence are inter-changed in passive voice.
- 3rd form of verb (past participle) will be used only (as main verb) in passive voice.

Auxiliary verbs for each tense are given below in the table.

Present Simple Tense (passive Voice) Auxiliary verb in passive voice: am/is/are	
Active voice: He sings a song. He does not sing a song. Does he sing a song?	Passive voice: A song is sung by him. A song is not sung by him. Is a song sung by him?

Simple Present Tense

Present Continuous Tense (passive Voice)
Auxiliary verb in passive voice: am being/is being/are being

Active voice: Passive voice:
I am writing a letter. - A letter is being written by me.
I am not writing a letter. - A letter is not being written by me.
Am I writing a letter? - Is a letter being written by me?

Present Perfect Tense (passive Voice)
Auxiliary verb in passive voice: has been/have been

Active voice: Passive voice:
She has finished his work. - Her work has been finished by her.
She has not finished her work. - Her work has not been finished by her.
Has she finished her work? - Has her work been finished by her?

Past Simple Tense (passive Voice)
Auxiliary verb in passive voice: was/were

Active voice: Passive voice:
I killed a snake. - A snake **was** killed by me.
I did not kill a snake. - A snake **was** not killed by me.
Did I kill a snake? - **Was** a snake killed by me?

Past Continuous Tense (Passive Voice)
Auxiliary verb in passive voice: was being/were being

Active voice: Passive voice:
He was driving a car. - A car **was being** driven by him.
He was not driving a car. - A car **was not being** driven by him.
They are playing football - Football **was being** played by them.

Past Perfect Tense (Passive Voice)
Auxiliary verb in passive voice: had been

Active voice: Passive voice:
They had completed the assignment. - The assignment **had been** completed by them.
They had not completed the assignment. - The assignment **had not been**

complete by them

Had they completed the assignment? - **Had** the assignment **been** completed by them?

Future Simple Tense (Passive Voice)
Auxiliary verb in passive voice: will be

Active voice: Passive voice:

She will buy a car. - A car **will be** bought by her.

She will not buy a car. - A car **will not be** bought by her.

Will she buy a car? - **Will** a car **be** bought by her?

Future Perfect Tense (passive Voice)
Auxiliary verb in passive voice: will have been

Active voice: Passive voice:

You will have started the job. - The job **will have been** started by you.

You will have not started the job. - The job **will not have been** started by you.

Will you have started the job? - **Will** the job **have been** started by you?

Note: The following tenses cannot be changed into passive voice.

1. Present perfect continuous tense
2. Past perfect continuous tense
3. Future continuous tense
4. Future perfect continuous tense
5. Sentence having Intransitive verbs

Examples:

1. Hari ate seven shrimp at dinner. (active)

At dinner, seven shrimp were eaten by Hari. (passive)

2. Beautiful giraffes roam the savannah. (active)
The savannah is roamed by beautiful giraffes. (passive)
3. Ravi changed the flat tire. (active)
The flat tire was changed by ravi. (passive)
4. I am going to watch a movie tonight. (active)
A movie is going to be watched by me tonight. (passive)
5. I ran the obstacle course in record time. (active)
The obstacle course was run by me in record time. (passive)
6. The crew paved the entire stretch of highway. (active)
The entire stretch of highway was paved by the crew. (passive)
7. Dad read the novel in one day. (active)
The novel was read by Dad in one day. (passive)
8. The critic wrote a scathing review. (active)
A scathing review was written by the critic. (passive)
9. I will clean the house every Sunday. (active)
The house will be cleaned by me every Sunday. (passive)
10. The staff is required to watch a safety video every year. (active)
A safety video will be watched by the staff every year. (passive)
11. She faxed her application for a new job. (active)
The application for a new job was faxed by her. (passive)
12. Ram painted the entire house. (active)
The entire house was painted by ram. (passive)
13. The teacher always answers the students' questions. (active)
The students' questions are always answered by the teacher. (passive)
14. The choir really enjoys that piece. (active)
That piece is really enjoyed by the choir. (passive)
15. Who taught you to ski? (active)
By whom were you taught to ski? (passive)
16. The forest fire destroyed the whole suburb. (active)
The whole suburb was destroyed by the forest fire. (passive)
17. The two kings are signing the treaty. (active)
The treaty is being signed by the two kings. (passive)
18. The cleaning crew vacuums and dusts the office every night. (active)
Every night the office is vacuumed and dusted by the cleaning crew. (passive)

19. Larry generously donated money to the homeless shelter. (active)
Money was generously donated to the homeless shelter by Larry. (passive)

20. No one responded to my sales advertisement (active)
My sales advertisement was not responded to by anyone. (passive)

Modal Auxiliary

1. Raja can write a poem

A poem can be written by Raja.

2. Raja must write a poem

A poem must be written by Raja.

3. Raja should write a poem

A poem should be written by Raja.

Interrogatives:

1.Will you hate me? Shall I be hated by you?

2. could you guide her? Could she be guided by you?

3. Do I love my friends? Are my friends loved by me?

Imperatives:

1. Open the window

Let the window be opened.

2. Submit the assignments

Let the assignments be submitted.

3. Shut your mouth

Let your mouth be shut

Impersonal Passive voice

1. Avoid cellphone while driving

Cellphone must be avoided while driving

2. Save enough money for future

Enough money should be saved for future.

Exercises:

1. The wedding planner is making all the reservations. (active)
2. Susan will bake two dozen cupcakes for the bake sale. (active)
3. The science class viewed the comet. (active)
4. Who ate the last cookie? (active)
5. Alex posted the video on Face book. (active)
6. The director will give you instructions. (active)
7. Thousands of tourists view the Grand Canyon every year. (active)
8. The homeowners remodeled the house to help it sell. (active)
9. The team will celebrate their victory tomorrow. (active)
10. The saltwater eventually corroded the metal beams. (active)

Answers:

1. All the reservations will be made by the wedding planner. (passive)
2. For the bake sale, two dozen cookies will be baked by Susan. (passive)
3. The comet was viewed by the science class. (passive)
4. The last cookie was eaten by whom? (passive)
5. The video was posted on Face book by Alex. (passive)
6. Instructions will be given to you by the director. (passive)

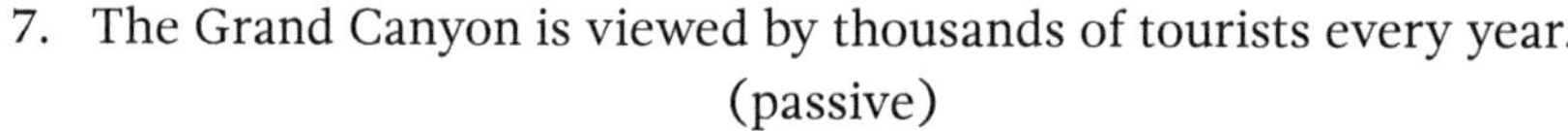

7. The Grand Canyon is viewed by thousands of tourists every year. (passive)
8. The house was remodeled by the homeowners to help it sell. (passive)
9. The victory will be celebrated by the team tomorrow. (passive)
10. The metal beams were eventually corroded by the saltwater. (passive)

Infinitive and Gerund

Gerunds and **infinitives** can replace a *noun* in a sentence.

Gerund = the present participle (-ing) form of the verb, e.g., singing, dancing, running.

Infinitive = to + the base form of the verb, e.g., to sing, to dance, to run.

Whether you use a **gerund** or an **infinitive** depends on the **main verb** in the sentence.

I expect *to have* the results of the operation soon. (Infinitive)

I anticipate *having* the research completed eventually. (Gerund)

Gerunds can be used after certain verbs including enjoy, fancy, discuss, dislike, finish, mind, suggest, recommend, keep, and avoid.

1. After *prepositions* of place and time.
   I made dinner *before getting* home.
   He looked unhappy *after seeing* his work schedule.
2. To replace the *subject or object* of a sentence
   Lachlan likes *eat**ing***coconut oil.
   *Jump**ing***off a cliff is dangerous, but a real thrill.

Infinitives can be used after certain verbs including agree, ask, decide, help, plan, hope, learn, want, would like, and promise.

1. After many *adjectives*:
   It is hard *to make* dinner this late.
   I find it difficult *to describe* my feelings about writing research essays.
2. To show *purpose*:
   I left for Russia *to study* Russian.
   I came to the office *to solve* the mystery of the missing keys.

Exercises:

1. Alan can't stand __________ on trains. (riding/ to ride)
2. Mr. Harris enjoys __________ people out to dinner. (inviting / to invite)
3. In the old days, gentlemen challenged their rivals ________. (fighting / to fight)
4. As the famous saying goes, there's no use _______ over spilt milk. (crying / to cry)
5. Jim stopped __________ his shoelace. Wait for him. (tying / to tie)
6. My wife always volunteers ____________ cakes PTA meetings. (baking / to bake)
7. Don't waste my time ____________ about your salary. (complaining/ to complain)
8. Eva is having trouble __________ on the exam. (concentrating / to concentrate)
9. Please allow me ______________ your Facebook page. (joining / to join)
10. You won't forget __________milk on your way home, will you? (picking up /to pick up)

Answers:

1. Riding 6. to bake
2. Inviting 7. complaining
3. to fight 8. concentrating
4. crying 9. to join
5. to tie 10. to pick up

Word Formation

It's crucial to understand how words change as they move from one portion of speech to the next. A noun such as beauty can be expressed as beautiful in adjective form, beautifully in adverb form, and beautify in verb form, for example. When we add suffixes and prefixes to the root word, this type of transformation occurs.

Verbs Nouns Adjectives Adverbs

1. Enable Ability Able Ably

2. Accept Acceptance acceptable Acceptably

3. Accuse Accusation Accusing Accusingly

4. Achieve Achievementachievable -

5. Act Act, Action, Activity Active Actively

6. Add Addition Additional Additionally

7. Admire Admiration Admirable Admirably

8. Advise Advice Advisable Advisably

9. Agree Agreement Agreeable Agreeably

10. Decide Decision Decisive Decisively

11. Distract Distraction Distracted Distractedly

12. Breathe Breath Breathless Breathlessly

13. Calm calm, calmness calm calmly

14. Care Care careful, caring carefully, carelessly

15. Clean Cleanliness Clean cleanly

16. Collect Collection Collective Collectively

17. Colour Colour Coloured Colourfully

18. Comfort Comfort Comfortable Comfortably

19. Complete Completion Complete Completely

20. Conclude Conclusion Conclusive Conclusively

21. Condition Condition Conditional Conditionally

22. Consider Consideration Considerable, Considerate Considerably

23. Criticize Critic Critical Critically

24. Custom Custom Customary Customarily

25. Destroy Destruction Destructive Destructively

Exercise:

I.**Attach a prefix to the word:**

1. Happy 2.Pure 3. Logical

4. Force 5. Famous 6. Hearted

7.Manage 8. Change 9. National

10. cautious

II. **Attach a suffix to the word:**

1.Sympathy 2. Internal

3.Violent 4. Triumph

5. Force 6. Refund

7. Attitude 8. Astronomy

9. Reflect 10. Laugh

III.Fill in the blanks with the appropriate forms of words.

Noun Adjective Verb

__________ Circulatory __________

__________ __________ Dispose

Economy __________ __________

__________ Emergent __________

__________ __________ Examine

Employment __________ __________

__________ Cultivable __________

Graduation __________ __________

__________ __________ Refer

Renewal __________ __________

Answers

I.Attach a prefix to the word:

1. **un**happy 2.**im**pure 3. **il**logical

4. **en**force 5. **in**famous 6. **wholeh**earted

7.**mis**manage 8. **inter**change 9. **inter**national

10. **over**cautious

II. **Attach a suffix to the word:**

1.Sympath**ise** 2. Internal**ly**

3.Violen**ce** 4. Triumph**ant**

5. Forc**ible** 6. Refund**able**

7. Attitud**inal** 8. Astronom**ical**

9. Reflect**ion** 10. Laugh**ter**

III.Fill in the blanks with the appropriate forms of words.

III.Fill in the blanks with the appropriate forms of words.

Noun Adjective Verb

Circulation Circulatory Circulate

Disposal Disposable Dispose

Economy **Economical Economize**

Emergency Emergent **Emerge**

ExaminationExaminable Examine

Employment **EmployableEmploy**

Cultivation Cultivable **Cultivate**

Graduation **GraduatedGraduate**

ReferenceReferale Refer

Renewal **RenewableReview**

Adverbs

A word or expression that modifies a verb, adjective, another adverb, determiner, clause, preposition, or sentence is referred to as an adverb. Adverbs are used to convey things like "how," "when," "where," and "to what extent?" Adverbs are used to express things like manner, place, time, frequency, degree, level of certainty, and so on. This is known as the adverbial function, and it can be carried out by single words (adverbs) or multi-word adverbial phrases and clauses.

Adverbs have long been considered one of the parts of speech. The English term adverb comes from the Latin adverbium, which is made up of the prefix ad- ("to"), verbum ("word", "verb"), and the noun suffix -ium. Adverbs' primary role, according to the term, is to act as modifiers of verbs or verb phrases. The manner, place, time, frequency, certainty, or other circumstances of the activity signified by the verb or verb phrase may be revealed by an adverb used in this way. Here are several examples:

- She sang loudly (loudly modifies the verb sang, indicating the manner of singing)
- We left it here (here modifies the verb phrase left it, indicating place)
- I worked yesterday (yesterday modifies the verb worked, indicating time)
- You often make mistakes (often modifies the verb phrase make mistakes, indicating frequency)

Adverbs can answer the types of questions about how an action was performed. They can also tell you when (We arrived early) and where (Turn here).

How?	**When?**	**Where?**	**How Often?**	**To What Extent?**
Angrily	Yesterday	Here	Almost	Always
Hungrily	Tomorrow	There	So	Never
Beautifully	Next week	Nowhere	Very	Often

However, there is one type of verb that doesn't mix well with adverbs. Linking verbs, such as feel, smell, sound, seem, and appear, typically need adjectives, not adverbs. A very common example of this type of mixup is

I feel badly about what happened.

Because "feel" is a verb, an adverb rather than an adjective seems appropriate. "Feel," on the other hand, isn't just any verb; it's a linking verb. An adjective explains what you feel, but an adverb tells how you do the activity of feeling. "I feel badly" denotes a lack of ability to sense emotions. It might make sense to state "I feel badly" if you're trying to read Braille while wearing thick leather gloves. "I feel bad," on the other hand, is the phrase to use if you're seeking to express negative feelings.

Adverbs can also be used to modify adjectives and other adverbs, and are frequently employed to denote degree. Examples:

- You are quite right (the adverb quite modifies the adjective right)
- She sang very loudly (the adverb very modifies another adverb – loudly)

Adverbs and sentences

- Some adverbs can modify entire sentences—unsurprisingly, these are called sentence adverbs. Common ones include *generally, fortunately, interestingly,* and *accordingly*. Sentence adverbs don't describe one particular thing in the sentence—instead; they describe a general feeling about all of the information in the sentence.
- Fortunately, we got there in time.
- Interestingly, no one at the auction seemed interested in bidding on the antique spoon collection.

At one time, the use of the word *hopefully* as a sentence adverb (e.g., *Hopefully, I'll get this job*) was condemned. People continued to use it though, and many style guides and dictionaries now accept it. There are still plenty of readers out there who hate it though, so it's a good idea to avoid using it in formal writing.

Placement of adverbs

Adverbs should be placed as near to the words they modify as possible. Placing the adverb incorrectly might result in an uncomfortable sentence at best, and a complete shift of meaning at worst. Only, which is one of the most frequently misplaced modifiers, should be avoided at all costs. Take a look at the following two sentences and compare them:

Example: Phillip only fed the cat.

Phillip fed only the cat.

The first statement implies that Phillip only did one thing: feed the cat. He didn't stroke the cat, pick it up, or do anything else with it. Phillip fed the cat, but not the dog, the bird, or anyone else who might have been there, according to the second phrase.

When an adverb is modifying a verb phrase, the most natural place for the adverb is usually the middle of the phrase.

Example:

We are quickly approaching the deadline.

Phillip has always loved singing.

I will happily assist you.

When to use adverbs and when to avoid them

Many people hold up Ernest Hemingway as an example of a superb writer who despised adverbs and recommended other authors to avoid them. In truth, it's hard to completely avoid adverbs. We all need them at times, and all authors (even Hemingway) need as well. The key is to avoid using adverbs that aren't necessary. Instead of looking for an adverb to give more colour to your verb or adjective when it doesn't seem powerful or specific enough, try reaching for a stronger verb or adjective. You'll almost always come up with a better word, and your work will be stronger as a result.

Examples:

- **Delicately**: Grandma's crystal vase is a priceless antique that must be handled **delicately**.
- **Delightfully**: Her outfit showcased her **delightfully** quirky personality.
- **Firmly**: The teacher **firmly** disciplined the students for their misbehavior.
- **Lightly**: She **lightly** dusted the brownies with a layer of powdered sugar before serving.
- **Truthfully**: She **truthfully** answered the police officer's questions.

Exercises:

1. He swims _____.
2. You _________ with the luggage while I find a cab.
3. He ran ______.
4. She spoke _________.
5. James coughed ________ to attract her attention.
6. He plays the flute _________. (after the direct object)
7. He ate the chocolate cake _________. (after the direct object)
8. __________ he returned home because he forgets the key at home.
9. ______ you rarely water the flowers?
10. Stop, if you are eating ________ quick.
11. Do you believe my mother _______?
12. We are talking ______ when we are disturbing by others.
13. He went ________ in Chennai for her business meetings.
14. _________, I have completed my graduation
15. Cats don't ________ walk backwards.
16. He ate the chocolate cake _______.

17. _______ does he use the ball?

18. The sentence __________ has a subject and a verb.

19. I ________ forget a face

20. My mother ______ watches TV at night.

Answers:

1. Well 2. Stay there

3. Quickly 4. Softly

5. loudly 6. Beautifully

7. greedily 8. Anxiously

9. could 10. Extremely

11. now 12.loudly

13. Somewhere 14.recently

15.Usually 16.Greedily

17.how often 18. Normally

19. Never 20.Seldom

CHAPTER THREE

UNIT III: PROBLEM SOLVING LETTER TO THE EDITOR

A letter to the editor (LTE) is a letter written to a publication regarding a topic that is important to the readers. Letters are usually written with the intention of being published. Letters to the editor can be written via conventional mail or electronic mail in many newspapers.

Newspapers and news magazines are the most common recipients of letters to the editor.

Letters to the editor cover a wide range of topics. However, the following are the most prevalent topics:

- Supporting or opposing the publication's editorial position, or reacting to another writer's letter to the editor.
- Commenting on a current topic under consideration by a governing body - whether local, regional, or national, depending on the circulation of the newspaper. Frequently, the writer will push elected officials to make decisions based on their own personal beliefs.
- Remarking on material from a prior publication (such as a news report). These letters might be either critical or laudatory.
- Correcting an error or misrepresentation that has been perceived.

Writing a Letter to the Editor

A letter to the editor is written in the format of a formal letter.

Sender's address: Give the sender's complete address.

Date: The date on which the letter is written comes next, immediately after the sender's address.

Receiver's address: The address of the recipient (the editor of the newspaper or magazine you intend to send your letter) should be written.

Subject line: The main purpose of the letter is mentioned in the subject line.

Salutation/Greeting: The salutation can be Sir, Ma'am, Respected Sir, Respected Ma'am, etc.

Body of the letter: The body of the letter should explain the purpose of the letter. Introduce yourself and provide all the details of the matter being discussed.

Complimentary closing: Thank you very much, Thank you or Thanking you can be the complimentary closing that you can use.**End the letter**: End the letter with your signature, name in block letters, and designation, if there is any.

Letter to the Editor Format

Formal letters format do not vary much in general,

Sender's Address

Date

Receiver's Designation

Address

Subject: ________________________________

Respected Ma'am/ Sir

Body of the Letter

Introduction- Gives a brief abstract of the content to follow.

Content- Includes the main details and subject matter of the letter.

Conclusion- This part concludes the information to provide a summary and give fluidity to the whole content.

A letter appears better structured if the writer adheres to this sequence of writing.

Yours Sincerely,

Sender's Name

Sender's Designation (Optional)

Sender's Signature

Example 1:

Sample Letter to the Editor to Highlight the Effects of Air Pollution

26 C, RMC nagar,
Chennai.
3rd, June, 2022
The Editor
The Indian Express
Chennai – 600023.

Subject: **Increase of air pollution in Chennai.**

Respected Sir/Ma'am,

I am suthosia, a member of NGO. I'm writing to inform you about the growing impact of air pollution in our neighborhood and the surrounding area.

Chennai has seen a significant expansion in the use of private transportation and the number of new industrial sectors in recent years. Breathing difficulties, chronic diseases, lung damage, nausea, exhaustion, and other major health risks have all increased as a result of this. Hospitals in the vicinity have already witnessed an unanticipated increase in the number of patients with chronic sickness symptoms, and it is critical that the public and government officials are made aware of this dangerous situation as soon as possible.

Because of the gravity of this situation, I respectfully request that you call attention to it so that steps can be made to reduce the impact of air pollution and the risk of people being impacted.

Thanking you
Yours sincerely,
Signature
SUTHOSIA RAJA
Member of NGO

Example 2:

Sample Letter to the Editor of a Newspaper to Highlight the Issue of Open Manholes

26 C, BSS Avenue,
RMC nagar,
Chennai.
3rd, June, 2022

The Editor
The Indian Express
Chennai – 600023.

Subject: Open Manholes on R S Road

Respected Sir/Ma'am,

I am Rathina Sabapathy, a resident of VKL Avenue. I'm writing to raise awareness about the problem of open manholes in our neighborhood.

These manholes have been open for more than 6 months, and there have been several accidents as a result of this. We've asked local governments and groups about this, but no action has been taken thus far, and it's becoming a major source of concern. Every day, children go to school, and many working people use this route since it connects the main road to the Electronic City region, where the majority of the IT companies are located.

Please think about this issue and write about it in your newspaper so that the authorities are aware of the need to investigate this scenario as soon as possible so that the number of casualties is minimized.

Thanking you
Yours sincerely,
Signature
RATHINA SABAPATHY S
Resident of VKL Avenue

Example 3:

Students can use this example to learn how to conduct offline exams in the face of rising COVID rates.

26 C, RMC nagar,
Chennai.
3rd, June, 2022

The Editor
The Indian Express
Chennai – 600023.

Subject: Conduction of Offline Examinations amidst the Increasing COVID Rates

Respected Sir/Ma'am,

I am Sathya Priya, a member of the Parent-Teacher Association. I'm writing to underline the importance of conducting offline assessments in schools and universities while the number of COVID cases is on the rise.

The fact that the disease is spreading faster than it has in the previous two years of the pandemic is cause for considerable concern, and it is not safe for us to send our children to their different schools and universities to take exams in this situation. We attempted to discuss the issue with academic institution authorities, but no action or decision has been taken thus far. In order to keep ourselves safe and healthy, we must exercise extreme caution and refrain from having any kind of physical contact with anyone.

I respectfully suggest that you recognize the gravity of this situation and publicize it in your newspaper so that academic institutions consider conducting online assessments to ensure everyone's safety.

Thanking you

Yours sincerely,

Signature

SATHYA PRIYA

Member of the Parent-Teacher Association

Example 4:

Sample Letter to the Editor Regarding Frequent Breakdown of Electricity.

26 C, RMC nagar,

Chennai.

3rd, June, 2022

The Editor

The Indian Express

Chennai – 600023.

Subject: Frequent Breakdown of Electricity

Respected Sir/Ma'am,

I am Dakshith Bala, a resident of RMC nagar. I've been living in RMC nagar with my family for almost 10 years, and we've never had any issues with electricity in our neighborhood. We have recently been having regular power outages lasting more than eight to nine hours.

The frequent power outages have a significant impact on day-to-day activities. The residents of the neighborhood have been inconvenienced greatly as a result of this. We don't know when we'll have power and when we won't, so no work happens as planned. Voltage fluctuations occur frequently; producing problems by disrupting the operation of commonly used electronic gadgets. This condition affects schoolchildren, working adults, women, and the elderly.

The Electricity Board's administrators must bear some responsibility for installing powerful transformers and streamlining the power supply. If you could spotlight the problem in a column of your renowned daily, it would be of tremendous assistance and relief to all of the inhabitants. We think that this will draw the attention of the authorities, and that action will be taken as soon as possible to alleviate the hardships we are experiencing as a result of the regular power outages.

Thank you for your time and consideration.

Yours sincerely,

Signature

DAKSHITH BALA

Resident of RMC nagar.

Exercises:

1.Write a letter to the Editor of The Times Newspaper, highlighting increasing technological addiction among the youth.

2. Write a letter to the editor of a daily newspaper to aware people on how stray animals can be COVID19 carriers and hence they must avoid direct contact.

3. Given the recent increase in road accidents and miss happenings, you are concerned about road safety. Write a letter to the editor of a popular magazine to showcase the same.

4. As a responsible citizen, you are concerned about the condition of Marine Lines. People have littered the entire place with plastic, masks and garbage. Write a letter to the editor of a leading daily to spread awareness on the matter.

5. Your school's/college's Yoga Club hosted a workshop called "Art of Living for Students." Write a letter to the editor of the local daily newspaper in roughly 100-120 words giving your thoughts on the matter.

Check List

A checklist is a form of task aid that is designed to prevent failure by correcting for human memory and attention limitations. It aids in the completion of a task by ensuring uniformity and completeness. The "to do list" is a simple example. A schedule, which lists things to be completed according to time of day or other factors, is a more advanced checklist. Documentation of the task and auditing against the documentation are two of the most important tasks in a checklist.

A written checklist can help you avoid skipping, omitting, or forgetting crucial tasks in any activity. The Effective Checklists have the following characteristics:

- Checklists should be easy to use and understand. Each item on the list should be required, and the group should be sufficient.
- Checklists that focus on a single person's tasks or a group of people who will collaborate are less likely to have items left off.
- Organizing tasks that may be completed at the same time, in the same place, or by the same person promotes efficiency.
- A checkbox may be present in a group to indicate that it has been completed. If there are numerous groups, this is more likely to be beneficial.
- The items to be checked by a specific individual might be grouped on the list whenever possible.
- Items should not be overly lengthy or unclear in their descriptions. Although crucial steps may be mentioned in order where order is relevant, a checklist should not attempt to define or describe operations that should be recognizable to the checker.
- The list should be arranged in a sensible order. When there is a need for chronological order, it should be specified by the order of the items in the list. An order that minimizes travel or search time is efficient when the things to be checked are spatially scattered.
- The most convenient and reliable checklists are usually completed in one sitting from top to bottom. It should be simple to recover from any interruption without the danger of missing an item or having to retake

a check.

- The physical checklist should be easy to utilize on the job. It shouldn't take any more effort to read it, and it shouldn't be protected from the elements.
- Cross-referencing to the standard method can be advantageous in some circumstances, especially for training and auditing.
- Some checklists must be signed and maintained as documentation, while others may be reused. This could have an impact on the format and materials.
- Checkboxes at the start of each item make it easy to locate and navigate to the following incomplete check. A keyword at the start of the text will aid in the selection of the correct box.
- A master checklist indicating the completion of each subordinate checklist may be used when numerous checklists are used due to the complexity of the work or the necessity for several individuals to complete checks at different locations.
- Instructions should be included if they are required. If not, they should be removed because they will cause the user to become distracted.

Format:

- Title of the check list.
- The interrogative form should be used
- Yes/No boxes should be provided for each question.
- The questions should begin with the 'do verb, to or to have' verb. .(Begin the questions with the auxiliaries such as is, are, do, does, and has/have)
- Put a tick mark in the 'yes' box when the item in question is made complete

Example 1:

Write down a check list containing at least eight items to avert fire accidents in public functions conducted in temporary structures.

Particulars Yes No

- Have I kept fire extinguishers ready? √ Have I instructed every one not to burn anything inside? √
- Have I checked whether the structure is strong? √
- Have I inspected whether any highly inflammable items are found inside? √
- Have I checked whether the electrical wires do not touch the structure? √
- Have I told everyone not to smoke inside? √
- Have I nominated some persons exclusively for checking the safety arrangements? √
- Have I informed the organizers not to put any enclosures? √

Example 2:

Checklist for an industrial Visit

Particulars Yes No

- Have I taken identity card? √
- Do I have the tickets safe? √
- Have I checked my health status with the doctor before travel? √
- Are all the documents taken? √
- Have I taken the confirmation letter? √
- Have I taken the visiting card of the Mumbai official? √
- Do I have enough money and the ATM card? √
- Have I taken my cell phone & charger? √
- Have I given necessary instructions to my team members? √

Example 3:

Checklist for an Interview

Particulars Yes No

- Have I taken identity card? √
- Do I have the tickets safe? √
- Are all the documents taken? √
- Have I taken all the certificates & testimonials? √
- Have I taken the Interview call letter? √
- Have I taken the visiting card of the Mumbai official? √
- Do I have enough money and the ATM card? √
- Have I taken my cell phone & charger? √
- Are all certificates arranged properly for easy reference? √
- Do I have a set of formal wear neatly packed? √
- Have I taken my project report? √

Example 4:

Write down a checklist containing at least eight items to avert fire accidents in public functions conducted in temporary structures.

Particulars Yes No

- Have I kept fire extinguishers ready? √
- Have I instructed the inmates not to burn anything inside the structure? √
- Have I checked the stability of the structure? √
- Have I checked the electrical connections? √
- Have I displayed 'No smoking' boards inside the structure? √
- Have I arranged for fire-engines to stand nearby? √
- Have I stored enough water to put out fire in the time of emergency? √
- Have I checked all other safety arrangements? √

Example 5:

Imagine that you are the student- secretary of English-club association. You have to organize the inaugural function of the association, Prepare a checklist of 8 items for the successful conduct of the function.

Particulars Yes No

- Have I decorated the auditorium? √
- Are the banners and posters displayed properly? √
- Have I assigned students to receive the chief guest? √
- Have I made the seating arrangement on the dais? √
- Have I checked the functioning of the PA system? √
- Have I prepared the order of events? √
- Are the student- volunteers informed of their duties? √
- Have I kept water bottles on the stage? √

Exercises:

1. Prepare an eight-item checklist for organizing a trip to Goa.

2. Prepare a checklist for conducting fresher's day in your college.

3. Prepare an eight-item checklist to organize the Pongal celebrations in your college.

4. Imagine that you have to attend an interview for any reputed Software Company in Bangalore next week. Prepare a checklist of eight items to make your interview a successful one.

5. Prepare an eight-item checklist for a foreigner who wants to visit India during the pandemic situation. 6. Write a Check List of eight points to maintain a pollution free environment in your college.

6. Prepare a checklist for conducting Annual day in your college.

7. Prepare an eight-item checklist for age old people going to hospital for health check-up in the Pandemic situation.

8. Imagine that you are Branch Manager of State Bank of India. You have been asked to attend a one day training program in Delhi. Prepare a checklist of eight important items that you have to check before starting the journey for the training program.

9. Write down a check list containing at least eight items to avert fire accident in the public conducted in temporary structures.

10. Write down a checklist highlighting at least eight items to arrange an inter collegiate cultural meet

Problem solution essay / Argumentative Essay

Problem-solving essays look at the issues that arise in a certain context and offer solutions to those issues. They resemble cause and effect essays in various aspects, particularly in terms of format (see below). Problem-solving essays are a subset of another sort of essay that includes the following four elements:

Situation

Problem

Solution

Evaluation

You must outline the problem and explain why it has to be solved in the introduction before presenting your solution. River pollution or youth gang issues are two examples of typical problem-solving essays. Include a problem description as well as statistical data or references. In most cases, a solution is presented after careful consideration. All instances of issues and solutions must include strong arguments and references.

Remember:

If it's a new problem, you'll have to describe it thoroughly.

If you're dealing with a well-known issue, you'll need to construct a vivid picture.

In both cases, you must persuade the reader that this is a significant issue.

Steps:

1. Describe the problem.

2. Explain the issue.
3. Persuade the reader that the issue requires attention.
4. Explanation of the proposed solution
5. Convince the reader that your solution is cost-effective and feasible
6. Make the case that this is the best option.
7. Dispute any objections.

Finding a Solution

Great solutions are:

- Implemented easily
- Effective at solving the problem
- Cost-effective
- Feasible

Structure:

A problem-solution essay can be structured in two ways. These are comparable to how cause and effect essays are structured, specifically using a block or chain structure. All of the problems are stated first, followed by all of the solutions in the block structure. Each problem is immediately followed by the answer to that problem in the chain structure. Both sorts of structures have advantages and disadvantages.

Block	Chain
Introduction (including 'situation')	Introduction (including 'situation')
Problem 1 Problem 2 ...	Problem 1 & Solution to Problem 1 Problem 2 & Solution to Problem 2 Problem 3 & Solution to Problem 3 ...
Transition sentence/paragraph	
Solution 1 Solution 2 ...	
Conclusion (including 'evaluation')	Conclusion (including 'evaluation')

STRUCTURE

Example 1:

Obesity and poor fitness

(block structure)

The increased use of processed and convenient meals, as well as our reliance on automobiles, has resulted in an increase in obesity and a decrease in adult fitness levels. Obesity affects one-third of the population in various countries, particularly those that are industrialised. This is relevant since obesity and poor fitness reduce life expectancy, thus it is critical for individuals and governments to collaborate to address this issue and improve citizens‘ diet and fitness.

Obesity and a lack of physical fitness shorten life expectancy. Obese persons are more likely to develop serious illnesses including diabetes and heart disease, both of which can lead to death. Regular exercise has long been known to minimize the risk of heart disease and stroke, thus persons with low fitness levels are at a higher risk of developing these conditions.

Individuals can extend their lives by altering their diet and increasing their physical activity. Today's society is reliant on the consumption of processed meals that are heavy in fat and sugar. People can make their diets healthier and more balanced by preparing their own food and eating more fruits and vegetables, which could lead to a decrease in obesity levels. People could choose to walk or cycle to work or the store instead of driving to enhance their fitness levels. They could also choose to walk up the stairs rather than take the elevator. These small improvements could result in a huge increase in fitness.

Governments could also take steps to enhance residents' food and physical activity habits. This could be accomplished through education, such as including classes on healthy eating and lifestyles in the curriculum. Governments may also do more to encourage individuals to walk or ride their bikes instead of driving, such as by constructing additional bike lanes or raising automobile charges. While some may argue that raising taxes is a bad strategy to handle the problem, it is no different than the high taxes imposed on cigarettes to curb smoking.

In short, obesity and poor fitness are major issues in modern society, resulting in decreased life expectancy. Individuals and governments can collaborate to address this issue and improve diet and fitness as a result. Individual solutions are more likely to have an impact than those proposed by the government; however it is evident that a coordinated effort with the government is required for success. With obesity levels in industrialized and industrializing countries continuing to rise, it is essential that we take action now to deal with this problem.

Example 2:

School Choice – An Educational Custom Fit

Consider what would happen if only one size of pant was sold in stores, and government restrictions prohibited the sale of any other size. This may sound weird, but it's really similar to what's going on with our country's children's education. As Indians, we have a lot of personal freedom, which happily includes the ability to choose the best-fitting clothes. Consider typical public education for a moment. The public school system has delivered a one-size-fits-all approach to educating our country's youngsters for decades. As the twenty-first century approached, the public education system began to show its age. In a fast changing environment typified by the emergence of personal computers and, later, the internet, and an increasing number of youngsters began to lag behind.

Many people began to urge for new educational models that would keep up with the times, sensing a need for change. The school choice movement got its start with this. Charter schools and school voucher programs are referred to collectively as "school choice" initiatives because they give parent the ability to pick specialized education options for their children outside of the traditional "one size fits all" public school system. A school voucher program provides parents with certificates that are used to pay for education at a school of their choice, rather than the public school to which they are assigned. Charter schools on the other hand are publicly funded schools that have been freed from inefficient public-school system rules and regulations in exchange for accountability to produce positive, measurable results.

Given the significance of public education, it's understandable that many people would be cautious to make changes. Opponents of school choice worry that public schools would be replaced by market-driven education firms that are more concerned with making a profit than with the individual education of pupils. Others express alarm over what appears to be government backing of private religious schools through various school voucher programs. Those who are opposed to school choice should be congratulated for their sincere concern for the education of our country's children, but the overwhelming data shows that school choice is the way to go in the future.

The focus on success through measured achievement and accountability is a hallmark of privately operated charter schools. Consider the one-size-fits-all trousers store: how long would they be in business if a competitor provided a variety of sizes and styles? Simply put, they couldn't, not when faced with competition that offers consumers more options. There was no competition for the old public school system in the past. There was no reason to improve the education they gave because there was nothing to compare it to. For the first time, the school choice movement provided an option to failing public schools. Charter schools make a promise, or charter, to attain a measurable level of educational performance within a set time frame.

It is obvious that the traditional one-size-fits-all approach to education is no longer appropriate. We must respond swiftly and accurately in steering our public education policies, given the new fast speed of the digital age. If we continue to cling to an outmoded system that produces terrible results, traditional public education will continue to yield poor results. A route of demonstrable results and accountability, on the other hand, should be pursued. Those who argue against school choice must be seen for what they are, which is nothing more than special interest protection, such as massive unions. Our nation, We must ensure that children will be provided with a choice-based education that is forward thinking, It is customized, fair to all citizens, and able to move into the future with them.

Exercises:

1.Money can't buy happiness.

2.Is Google making us stupid?

3.Immigration

4.College sports

5. How do social media lead to isolation?

Error correction

Detecting errors is a talent that comes in handy all the time, whether you're a student taking an English exam in school, a government exam, the SAT, or any other English proficiency exam. To be successful in error spotting, a candidate must have a strong command of English grammar and vocabulary. You must find an error in the sentences provided in error spotting. Nouns, pronouns, or any other grammatical problem in the sentence can be the source of the error.

Example:

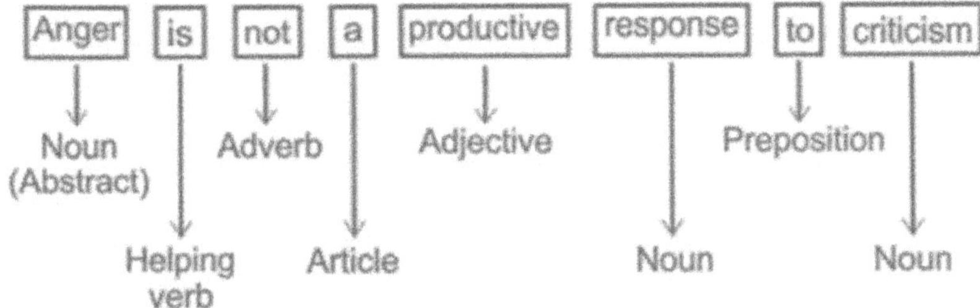

Nouns:

A noun is a word that describes a place, person, or object. It can be singular or plural, however the verbs used for singular and plural are different.

For example: Police, clergy, people, peasantry, animals, and other singular nouns represent plurality and take a plural verb in a sentence.

Clothes, Scissors, Trousers, Amends, Spectacles, and other nouns take the plural verb because of their plural form.

When a noun signifying weight, number, money, length, or measure appears after a number, the noun form does not change as long as another noun or pronoun appears after it, for example, million, pair, meter, year, dozen.

Pronouns

In the instance of possession, a pronoun is a term that refers to the noun in the phrase.

When using the pronoun 'one,' make sure to keep it throughout the phrase.

'Whose' is normally used for living people, while 'which' is used for non-living things.

Adjectives

An adjective is a word which represents the specialty, merits, demerits, quality and fault of a person, place or thing.

- Instead of 'who' or 'which', the relative pronoun 'that' is used after adjectives in the superlative degree
- 'As' is used both before and after the adjective to show equality.

Adverbs

An adverb is a word that changes the meaning of a noun or a verb. Some of the adverbs have the same meaning, causing people to be perplexed. Less and fewer are two of these words. ‘Fewer’ is used to indicate quantity, whereas ‘Less’ is used to indicate number and adjectives such as little, a little, and the little are employed in distinct contexts.

Example 1:

The format of the different words in the sentence that serve the same function should be the same.

All students should be learning word processing, accounting and **computer programming.** (Correct)
All students should be learning word processing, accounting, and **how to program computers.**(Incorrect)

Example 2:
Modifiers are used to change the subject and must be placed next to it. As a result of their actions, the meaning of the sentence is altered.

Covered in mud, Mark helped the puppy. (Incorrect)
Covered in mud, the puppy was helped by Mark. (Correct)

Example 3:

The right words should be used in the right situations.

See you later (Correct)
See you latter (Incorrect)

Example 4:

Repetition of the same concept is unnecessary.

She will return back on Tuesday. (Incorrect)
She will return on Tuesday. (Correct)

Example 5:

In a sentence, 'though‘ is always followed by 'yet,‘ not 'but.‘

Though he is rich but he is kind. (Incorrect)
Though he is rich, yet he is kind. (Correct)

Example 6:

'Not' is never used with 'unless' because 'unless' expresses a condition that is always used in the negative sense

Unless you do not pay the fine, you will not be excused.(Incorrect)
Unless you pay the fine, you will not be excused. (Correct)

Example 7:

'While' represents the length of time spent doing something, while 'When' denotes a broad meaning (general sense).

When learning how to box, the technique is of utmost importance.(Incorrect)
While learning how to box, the technique is of utmost importance. (Correct)

Example 8:

Punctuation - For the sentence to make sense, punctuation is more necessary. Candidates who do not understand punctuation may miss the error.

It's a beautiful garden (correct)

Its a beautiful garden (incorrect)

Tips to improve:

- Reading is a great approach to improve your grammar. Good books and English publications, such as The Hindu and The Times of India, should be read.
- Look at some basic grammar books.

- Before answering, read the statement carefully and perhaps more than once.
- Make an effort to comprehend the meaning, goal, and message of the language being communicated to the reader.
- Practice and practice because they say that practice makes perfect, right? You can prepare for the exam by using previous year's papers and mock examinations.
- Finally, do not be concerned about the exam. When you're feeling overwhelmed, take a deep breath, relax your thoughts, and try again.

Exercises:

We have provided some questions so that you may practice all that you have learnt. Spot the errors in the sentences given below –

1. Chemistry is nisha's favourite subject (A)/.It comes as a shock(B)/ to everyone in the class(c)/ selling him fail in it(d).
2. We hope so you'll come in Newyork soon.
3. Sheela works like a waitress on Friday.
4. The price of living is very high in Chennai.
5. I am born in Mumbai.
6. Would you like to have some desert?
7. Raja is married with kamatchi.
8. My aunt will arrive at Tuesday.
9. Ramesh shot the bird by a gun.
10. Myself I am raja.
11. Dolphins and killer whales has learned elaborate routine to entertain aquarium audiences. They are thought by men to being even more scientifically intelligent then me. In scientific experiments they had showed great skill for distinguishing between objects.

Answers:

1.The error lies in B. Comes which is in the simple present tense is grammatically incorrect as per the sentence construction.(has come)

2. We hope so you'll come **to** Newyork soon.

3. Sheela works **as** a waitress on Friday.

4. The **cost** of living is very high in Chennai.

5. I **was** born in Mumbai.

6. Would you like to have some **dessert**?

7. Raja is married **to** kamatchi.

8. My aunt will arrive **on** Tuesday.

9. Ramesh shot the bird **with** a gun.

10. I am Raja.

11.Dolphins and killer whales **have** learned elaborate routine to entertain aquarium audiences. They are thought by men to **be** even more scientifically intelligent **than** me. In scientific experiments they had **shown** great skill **in** distinguishing between objects.

If – Conditionals

A sentence including a conditional clause is known as a conditional sentence. If or unless (if...not) is frequently used to introduce a conditional sentence, which indicates a condition or presumption

Examples:

If you call him, he'll come.

He'll come if you call him.

Unless it rains, we won't postpone the match.

We won't postpone the match unless it rains.

There are 3 main types of conditional sentences which are distinguished by the tenses used in the conditional clause and the main clause. There is also a zero type.

The basic structure of conditional clauses is given below:

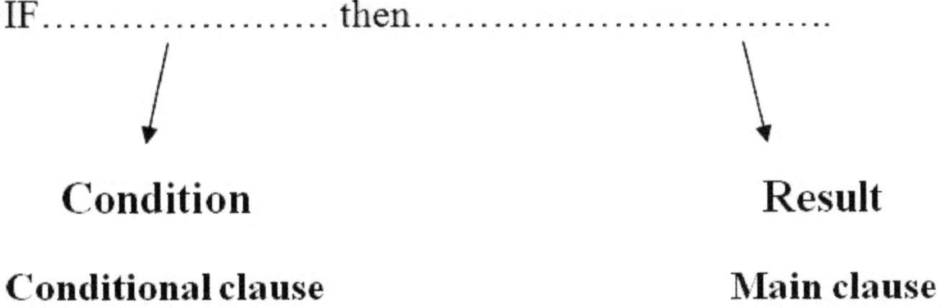

Basic Structure of Conditional Clauses

Type 1 – Probable conditions

Conditional clause	Main clause
Simple present/present progressive/ present perfect/ Should +infinitive	Will/shall/can/may+infinitive
If my sister comes,	She'll help you
If he has finished,	He can go
If you want to lose weight,	You will probably be hungry
If you should phone him,	He'll come in the morning

Type 1 condition is an open condition. It refers to what is likely to happen in the present or future.

Note:

1. In the main clause, we can use the word 'should.'

If you are going to London, you should have visit the British museum

1. When we make a request, we can utilize 'will' in the conditional clause.

If you will learn English, I'll be grateful.

3. We can eliminate 'if' when using the word 'should.'

Should you find my wallet, you will call me immediately.

4. We can use 'would like to' and 'would care to' meaning 'want' or 'wish'.

If you would like to buy there, my daughter will help you.

5. We can use the imperative in the main clause.

If you see my brother, give him this gift.

Type 2 – Improbable conditions/ Rejected conditions:

Simple Past	Would/should/could/might +infinitive
If you called him,	He would come
If we followed him,	We would find a house
If I were you,	I would accept these conditions
If he worked hard,	He would pass the exam.
If I had wings,	I would fly

Type 3 – Impossible and Hypothetical conditional

Past perfect	Would/Could/might +have+third form of the verb
If you had told me before,	I could have got you the tickets.
If you had worked hard,	You would have passed the exam.
If she had helped him,	He would have got the job.
If he had known it before,	He would have applied for the job
If they had played well,	They would have won the match

Zero type:

If you press the button, the machine starts.

If I have a time, I go for a walk.

Inversions in the conditional sentences:

In Type 1(should inverted)

Should my mother call me tell her I'm not feeling well.

Type 2 (were to inverted)

Were they to arrive tomorrow we would have to buy some mangoes.

Type 3 (past perfect inverted)

Had you seen what I saw you would have also believe it

Other expressions used in conditional clause

Whether …. Or not	Whether you pay or not, you won't get in without an invitation
On condition that Provided that Providing that So long as As long as Assuming that Supposing that	I will tell my age on condition that you tell yours. What would you ask supposing that you were given the chance to see the God? Assuming that it's fine tomorrow, we'll go for a game.

Exercises:

I. **Complete the sentence:**

1. If it was dangerous, ________________
2. If I pass my driving test,_________________
3. _________________________, you would spend money on fuel.
4. _________________________, I'll tell her.
5. _______________________, she wouldn't be working as a receptionist.
6. If you worked hard, ___________.
7. If ______________________, he will see the Tajmahal.
8. ________________________, you will be selected.
9. What would you happen,____________?
10. Look me up ___________.

II.Rewrite each conditional sentence in the other two types.

1.If I finish my work, I'll come	If I finished my work, I would come	If I had finished my work, I would have come.
2.If I have time, I'll visit him		
3.	If the teacher had time, she would help you.	
4.If he works hard, he will pass the exam		
5.		If I had the money, I would have bought the car

III.Fill in the blanks with the right form of the verbs in the following sentences.

1. If he __________(teach) in the class, his result ______(not be) so poor.
2. If he______(eat) all that he will be ill.
3. If she had money, she ______(buy) gold ornaments.
4. If I ________(see) a ghost now, I _________(scream) at the top of my voice for help.
5. The table will collapse if you _________(stand) on it.

Answers:

I.**Complete the sentence**:

1.If it was dangerous, **I would talk to her.**

2.If I pass my driving test, **I'll buy a car.**

3.**If you bought a car**, you would spend money on fuel.

4.**If I see her**, I'll tell her.

5. **If she were rich**, she wouldn't be working as a receptionist.

6.If you worked hard, **you could pass the exam.**

7. **If Rajesh goes to Agra**, he will see the Tajmahal.

8.**If you called for the interview**, you will be selected.

9.What would you happen, **if you kicked the ball?**

10. Look me up **if you happen to come this side next time.**

II.

1.If I finish my work, I'll come	If I finished my work, I would come	If I had finished my work, I would have come.
2.If I have time, I'll visit him	**If I had time, I would visit him.**	**If I had had time, I would have visited him.**
3. **If the teacher has time, she will help you.**	If the teacher had time, she would help you.	**If the teacher had had time, she would have helped you.**
4.If he works hard, he will pass the exam	**If he worked hard, he would pass the exam**	**If he had worked hard, he would have passed the exam**
5. **If I have the money, I will buy the car.**	**If I had the money, I would buy the car.**	If I had the money, I would have bought the car

III.

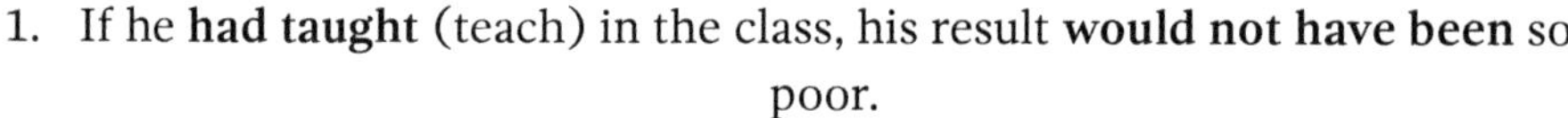

1. If he **had taught** (teach) in the class, his result **would not have been** so poor.
2. If he **eats** (eat) all that he will be ill.
3. If she had money, she **would have bought** (buy) gold ornaments.
4. If I **saw** a ghost now, I **would scream** at the top of my voice for help.
5. The table will collapse if you **stand** on it.

Compound words

A compound is generated when two words are combined to form a new meaning.

Open compounds (spelled as two words, e.g., high school), closed compounds (combined to form a single word, e.g., doorknob), and hyphenated compounds are the three types of compound words (two words joined by a hyphen, e.g., long-term). A compound can sometimes consist of more than two words (e.g., father-in-law).

For example, you could make the compound word "inside" by combining the words "in" and "side."

We should play **inside** today.

The words "carry" and "over" can be used to form the compound word "carry over."

We can **carry over** that surplus into the next sprint.

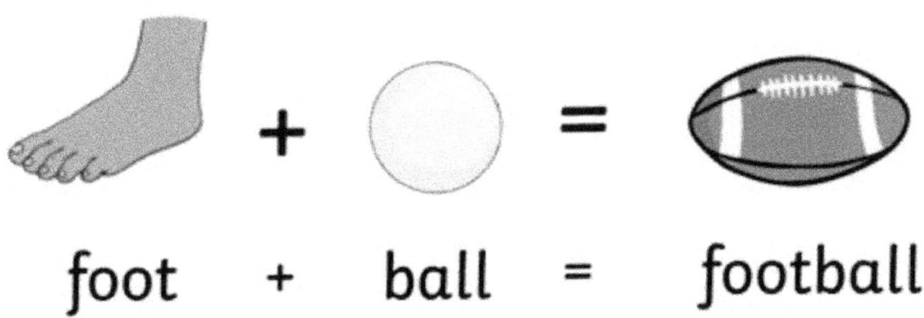

Compound word

List of compound words

Bullfrog Snowball Mailbox

Anybody Football Grandmother

Outside Firefighter Railroad

Notebook Sometimes Breakfast

Superhero Waistcoat Sunflower

Cannot Armchair Toothbrush

Mailbox Skateboard Lipstick

Living room Full moon Long-term

Carryover Real estate Mother-in-law

Waterfall Ice cream Good-hearted

Backstage Hot dog Merry-go-round

Bookstore Bookend Check-in

backlog Sidekick Battleship

Raincoat Fishbowl Coffeemug

Peanut butter No one Largelyirrelevant

Exercises:

Which of the words given below can be placed after the word given in Bold to form a compound word :

1.Skate....

a. school b. light c.board

2. Sun....

a. flower b.rose c.thing

3. grand

a. tooth b.jury c. dog

4.full

a. sister b. moon c. in

5. home

a. wash b. line c.made

6. life

a. step b.long c.step

7. boy

a. life b.scouts c. tooth

8. soft

a.sofa b.ball c.step

9. sea

a.food b.shell c.both

10. earth

a. stick b.long c.worm

Answers:

1.board 2.flower

3.jury 4.moon

5.made 6.long

7. scouts 8.ball

9. both 10.worm

Sentence completion

Sentence completions assess the ability to fill in the blanks in complex and incomplete sentences. It assesses a candidate's vocabulary and ability to understand sentence logic. These are frequently lengthy sentences.

There are possibly **four types** of sentence completions:

Restatement: Containing words such as namely, in other words, in fact, that is, etc.

Example: The pickpocket was a trickster, in other words, a _______.

Here answer will be **knave or scoundrel**, which restates "trickster,"

Comparison: Containing the words such as likewise, similarly, and, just as, as like as, etc.

Example: Jack was cleared of all charges; similarly, Jill was _______.

Here we have to compare 'cleared of all charges' with the suitable word, and hence **vindicated** is the answer.

Contrast: Containing the words such as though, although, however, despite, but, yet, on the other hand, but, however, despite, or, on the contrary, etc.

Example: Although the tiger is a solitary beast, its cousin the lion is a _______ wild animal.

Here answer should be in contrast with "solitary". Therefore, **gregarious or sociable** are possible answers.

Cause and effect: Containing words such as this, therefore, consequently, because of, etc. Also contains phrases such as due to, as a result, leads to, etc.

Example: A truck stole her parking spot; consequently, Rocky's _______ look showed her displeasure.

Here answer should be to find the cause for someone to steal. Therefore answer may be **scowling or sullen.**

Tips:

1.Read the sentence:

By reading carefully, you can use the sentence hints. Because of the complex words and phrase style, the question may be challenging. If you don't deconstruct the statement to see what suits best, you won't be able to answer the question even if you know the meanings of the words.

2. **Hints:**

The hints may help you figure out what should go in the blank for a coherent phrase. Here's a test to see if you can find the proper tip. If we alter the hint, we must also change the option in the blank. We can test the tip by typing that word or phrase directly into the blank.

3. **Pluses and Minuses:**

Once we find the word clues, indicate the kind of word we are now looking for with positive meaning or negative meaning. Also, to indicate synonyms or antonyms, we can use these symbols.

Examples:

1.A diamond ring is the _______ symbol of love and affection.

a. precocious b. fugacious c. **quintessential**

2.With the curtains drawn back, the room was _______ with warm sunlight.

a. recessed b. intruded c. **suffused**

Exercises:

1. Suresh's skin was _______ to burn if he spent too much time in the sun.

a. Prone b. Eminent c. Erect

2. The Security officer _______ the crowd to step back from the fire to avoid any mishappening.

a. Undulated b.Enjoined c. Stagnated

3. The college professor was known on campus as a _______ character—bland but harmless and noble in his ideals.

a. staid b. stagnant c.auspicious

4. Because he was so _______, the athlete was able to complete the obstacle course in record time.

a. belligerent b. nimble c. demure

5. The toy store's extensive inventory offered a _______ of toys from baby items to video games for teenagers.

a. manifold b. lexicon c. gamut

6. With sunscreen and a good book, April _______ by the pool in her lounge chair while the children swam.

a. ensconced b. sustained c. lolled

7. Dogs growl and show their teeth in an attempt to _______ the animal or person they perceive as a threat.

a. bolster b. waylay c. cow

8. The battalion's _______ was a well-fortified structure near the enemy lines.

a. labyrinth b. summary c. garrison

9.The enormous waves forced the lobster boat to _______ heavily to the starboard side, causing crates of lobsters to topple and fall into the ocean.

a. trifle b. degenerate c. list

10. Walking through the _______ forest in spring was a welcome escape from the cold, gray winter we had spent in the city.

a. pliant b. verdant c. factious

11.Must we be subjected to your _______ complaints all day long?

a. tiresome b. fearsome c. awesome

12.The _______ newspaper accounts of the city scandal caused some readers to question the truth of the stories.

a. lurid b. vivacious c. blithesome

13. The _______ man with amnesia was unable to recognize where he was.

a. endogenous b. euphoric c. nonplussed

14. At the beginning of the ceremony, the high school band _______

the arrival of the graduates by playing the alma mater loudly and with enthusiasm.

a. decried b. heralded c. permeated

15. Although Sophie was afraid of heights, she seemed to have no _______ about driving over bridges.

a. enormity b. qualms c. imminence

16.I will write a rough draft of the proposal, and then you can edit it for any _______ material so that it is as convincing and concise as possible.

a. grandiose b. incontrovertible c. extraneous

17. The meeting is _______; everyone must attend.

a. palatable b. compulsory c. reciprocal

18. Through the _______ act of volunteering, it is possible to make a difference in the lives of the less fortunate.

a. dilatory b. insurmountable c. noble

19. The proposed design includes many _______ features that are not functional and can be eliminated to cut costs.

a. jovial b. germane c. extrinsic

20. There is no way around it: plagiarism is _______ to thievery.

a. tantamount b. apathetic c. fatuous

21.I am _______ of the problems that this solution will cause, but I still believe that this is the best possible solution.

a. innocuous b. cognizant c. precipitous

22. Because of the _______ of reliable information, Quentin's report was comprised mostly of speculation.

a. dearth b. diatribe c. myriad

23.The palace's great hall was rich in history and splendor, the walls hung with _______ tapestries.

a. mellifluous b. malleable c. ornate

24. After weeks of heavy rains, the earth gave way; mud and trees_______ down the mountain swallowing cars and houses in their path.

a. hurtled b. inculcated c. aspersed

25. The _______ butter had been left in the refrigerator for years.

a. complacent b. scandalous c. rancid

26. Several weeks of extremely hot, dry weather _______ the land, so instead of rowing across a river, we walked across a cracked, parched riverbed.

a. oscillated b. desiccated c. subverted

27.The task of building the cabin was a _______ one, but Rob was up to the challenge.

a. laborious b. venerable c. archaic

28. After the neighbor's stereo woke her up for the fifth night in a row, Brenda felt _______ to complain.

a. impelled b. rebuked c. augmented

29. Carter is writing a letter of recommendation that I can include in my _______ for prospective employers.

a. denunciation b. panacea c. dossier

30. _______ laughter came from the upstairs apartment where Trang was having a graduation party.

a. Scurrilous b. Deleterious c.Uproarious

Answers:

1. Prone
2. Enjoined
3. Staid
4. Nimble (adj.) is quick and light in movement, to be agile.
5. A gamut (n.) is an entire range or a whole series.
6. To loll

7. To cow (v.) is to intimidate, frighten with threats or show of force.
8. A garrison (n.) is a fort or outpost where troops are stationed; any military post.
9. To list (v.) (related to a vessel) is to incline or to cause to lean to one side.
10. Verdant (adj.)
11. Tiresome (adj.) mean
12. Lurid (adj.) means glaringly sensational or vivid; shocking.
13. Nonplussed (adj.) means greatly perplexed, filled with bewilderment
14. To herald (v.) is to proclaim or announce; to foreshadow.
15. A qualm (n.) is a sudden or disturbing feeling.
16. Extraneous (adj.)
17. Compulsory (adj.)
18. Noble (adj.) means having high, selfless moral standards; of
19. Extrinsic (adj.)
20. Tantamount (adj.)
21. Cognizant (adj.)
22. Dearth (n.)
23. Ornate (adj.) means richly and artistically finished or stylized.
24. To hurtle (v.) is to rush with great speed; to move violently with great noise; to fling forcefully.
25. Rancid (adj.) means rotten or putrid.
26. To desiccate (v.)
27. Laborious (adj.)
28. To impel (v.) is to motivate; push or drive forward; propel.
29. A dossier (n.) is a collection of papers giving detailed information about a particular person or subject.
30. Uproarious (adj.)

CHAPTER FOUR

UNIT IV: REPORTING OF EVENTS AND RESEARCH RECOMMENDATIONS

In both technical and general fields, recommendations are frequently employed. One can provide recommendations to other users. This will aid them in the upkeep of anything, the observance of specific safety precautions, and so forth. This work of writing suggestions is critical for technocrats who must constantly provide their important guidelines in order to complete duties properly.

Recommendations are advice given on a certain topic. The difference between a recommendation and an instruction is that a recommendation is more like a suggestion, while an instruction is more like an order that must be followed. You are not required to follow the advice. It's only a suggestion.

The following are some useful expressions for making recommendations:

It is necessary that

It is suggested/ recommended/ advised

It is important

It is necessary to

It is imperative

It is mandatory

It is desirable

It is essential that

It is indicated, proposed, or advised.
It is required.
I would likely to be
Need to be, etc.

Examples:

1. **Write a set of eight recommendations to save water.**

a. Instead of using water for cleaning, restaurants might save water by using paper plates and napkins.
b. We should turn off the tap when we don't need it and not leave it running when we don't need it.
c. It is recommended that the pipelines be checked on a regular basis to seal any leaks that may occur.
d. It is advised that new dams be built to save the water that we receive during rainstorms.
e. Roof-top rain collection is required to replenish the subsurface water – table.
f. It's critical to build check dams across canals and streams.
g. We need to learn to use water wisely.
h. Always keep in mind that water is the elixir of life.
a. It is recommended not to leave water running
j. We should skip the long showers.
k. It is advised to use a sprinkler system.
ax. Use your automatic washing machine only for full loads only
all. Don't run the hose while washing your car
n. Don't play too much with water in the summer.
o. We should try to reuse our rainwater.
p. Install water-saving aerators on all of your faucets.

2. **Recommendations to save petrol**

a) Keep the engine in good working order to save money on gas.
b) A high-mileage engine should be installed in a vehicle.
c) When the car is not moving, we should not leave the engine running.
d). To save petrol, avoid shifting gears frequently.
e). The air pressure in the tyres should be set to the recommended level.
f). The engine oil must be changed on a regular basis.
g). The vehicle should be serviced on a regular basis, because a poorly maintained vehicle uses more gasoline.

h). Clutch driving should be avoided.

i) Clean the air filter regularly

j) Clean Out the Trunk and Eliminate Unnecessary Weight

k)It is advised not to buy Premium Fuel.

l) Encourage Drivers to Observe Posted Speed Limits.

m) Encourage Carpooling.

n) It is recommended filling the tank in the morning.

o) Don't drive if it's raining.

3. **Recommendations to avoid Air Pollution.**

a. When purchasing a new car, consider one that is the most efficient, lowest-polluting vehicle or even a zero-emission electric car.
b. It is recommended to ride a bike when possible.
c. It is advisable to use public transportation.
d. Organize and condense errands into one trip.
e. When driving, accelerate gradually and obey the speed limit.
f. It is advisable to plant trees.
g. Maintain your vehicle and keep the tires properly inflated.
h. Use Recycle paper, plastic, metals and organic materials.
a. Should avoid crackers in the function
j. It is always better to build industries and railway stations far away from residential areas.

Exercises:

1. Write a set of eight recommendations to solve unemployment in India.
2. Write a set of eight recommendations that will help the public to follow traffic rules.
3. Write a set of eight recommendations to improve the English Language skills.
4. Write a set of eight recommendations for educating children in rural areas
5. Write a set of eight recommendations to prevent fire accidents.

Transcoding

An important study skill is the ability to transfer knowledge from verbal to visual and visual to verbal. One of the most important aspects of professional writing is transcoding. A couple of illustrations may make any report more fascinating. Visual representation is an added advantage to any presentation. There are two categories of visuals, namely figures and tables. Figures may be further classified into graphs, maps, charts, etc.,

Some Examples of Graphics:

Line Graph/Chart : To observe the relationship between two related phenomena.

Bar chart / Histogram : To compare two or more facts with reference to a particular item.

Flow chart: Narrative writing of different stages on development of a process.

Pie chart : Proportion of distribution of components, facts or progress within a given total situation.

Tabular column: When more than one parameter is compared with a number of items is involved.

Tree diagram: To show the historical nature of dependent processes.

Procedure for Transcoding:

- Observe the given chart/table
- Understand the idea/meaning
- Interpret the infer messages from the figures.
- Prepare rough draft
- Arrange it logically.
- Begin the paragraph with topic sentence

- Use discourse markers (discourse markers are expressions that are used to show how discourse is constructed).
- Show the connections between what a speaker is saying and what has already been said or what is going to be said.

Tips for writing:

Balancing contrasting Points: On the other hand, while, whereas

Emphasizing a contrast: However, nevertheless, still, yet, inspite of

Similarity: Similarly, in the same way

Counter – argument: However, even so, but, etc.,

Structuring: First(ly), second(ly), first of all, lastly, etc.,

Adding : Moreover, furthermore, in addition to, as well as that, besides, in any case,

Generalizing: On the whole, in general, broadly speaking, to a great extent, to some extent, apart from, except for...

Giving Examples: for instance, for example, in particular,

Logical consequence: Therefore, as a result, so, then, consequently,

Examples:

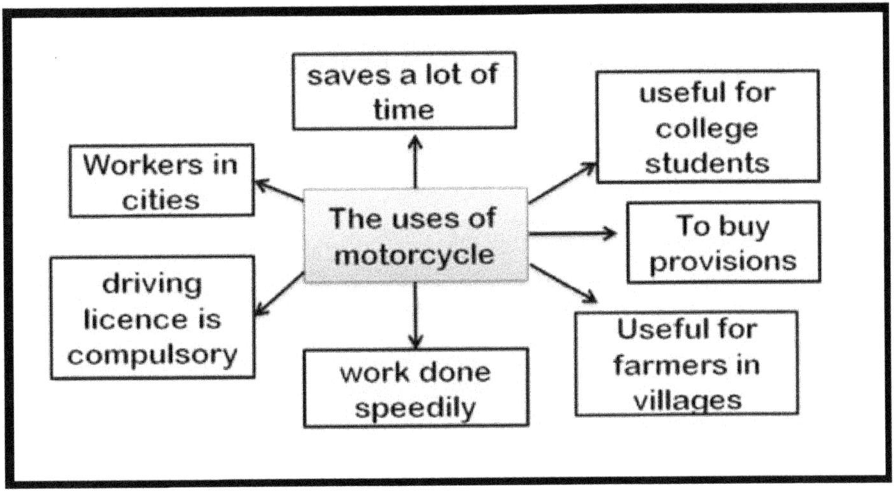

The Uses of Motorcycle

The motorcycle has evolved into a versatile vehicle that can be used not just in cities but also in rural areas. For starters, it saves a significant amount of time. Even in small towns and villages, it is highly handy for college students who need to travel great distances rather than relying on infrequent bus services. Many people keep motorcycles in their towns and cities for their servants to go out and buy food. Motorcycles are often used by city workers and even farmers in rural areas. This is due to the motorcycle's ability to expedite the work. Of course, a driver's licence is required to operate a motorcycle. To avoid serious injuries, one should also wear a helmet and drive carefully.

2. Your school plans an exhibition to display the neighboring states of Maharashtra. The following is the information given in the form of a table. Write two paragraphs of about 70 to 80 words using information given below.

Aspects	Maharashtra	Karnataka
Area	3,07,713 sq km	1,91,791 sq km
Population	7,89,37,187	4,49,77,209
Capital	Mumbai	Bangalore
Language	Marathi	Kannada
Rivers	Godawari,Krishna, Bhima,Koyana etc.	Tungabhadra, Kaveri etc.
Crops	Jawar, Bajara, Sugarcane,	Jawar,Tea,Rubber
Major Cities	Mumbai, Nagpur, Aurangabad,Nasik etc.	Bangalore,Hubli,Dharwad etc.

Maharashtra is not the same as Karnataka, but both are the states of India. Maharashtra covers 3,07,713 square kilometres, while Karnataka covers 1,91,791 square kilometres. The languages spoken in each region are almost entirely distinct. In Maharashtra, Marathi is spoken, while in Karnataka, Kannada is spoken. Godavari, Krishna, Bhima, and Koyana are prominent rivers in Maharashtra, whereas Tungabhadra and Kaveri are important rivers in Karnataka.

Jawahar's main crop is bajara, while Maharashtra's main crop is sugarcane, and Karnataka's main crop is tea and rubber. Mumbai, Nagpur, Aurangabad, Nasik are the major cities in Maharashtra, while Bangalore, Hubli, Dharwad, and other cities in Karnataka are the significant cities. Mumbai is Maharashtra's capital city, while Bangalore is the state capital of Karnataka. Maharashtra's population is 7,89,37,187 people, while Karnataka's population is 4,49,77,209.

3. **Advantages of watching TV**

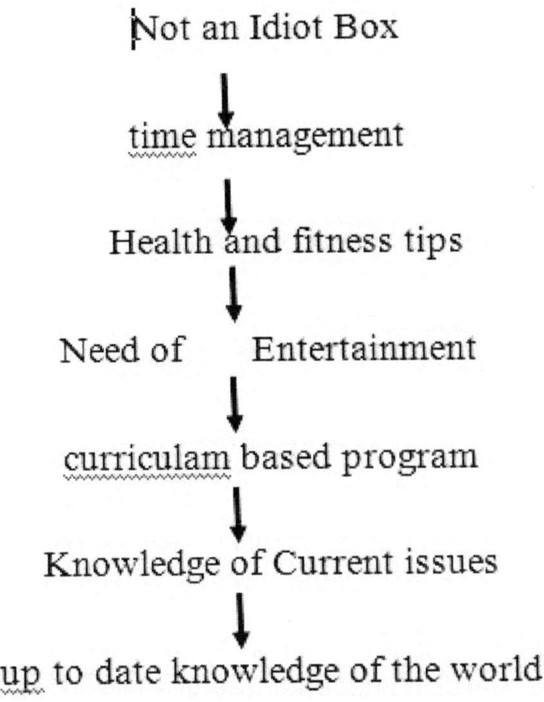

A pleasure of watching Television

Some individuals believe that television is the source of all evils, while others consider it to be their best friend. Some people attribute society's violence, consumerism, and disinformation to television, while others see it as a rich resource for education and global understanding. In my point of view, watching television has a number of advantages. When we catch it jointly, it helps to increase family togetherness. It keeps us informed about current events.

Television shows, music, video songs, live matches, and other forms of entertainment are available to us. We can learn how to make a few dishes by watching culinary shows. Teleshopping aids in the acquisition of low-cost deals. By watching television, we can keep up with the current fashion trends. By watching a variety of things on television, we may also learn how to manage 7 times in our lives. Channels like Discovery, National Geographic, Science Channels, and others provide us with a wealth of information.

By watching unique episodes designed for children, children can acquire moral lessons in an entertaining way. It also helps us to be fit and healthy because we may watch fitness-related programs and obtain fitness recommendations from it. Spiritual shows can help us develop our character. We become aware of our country's and the world's current socioeconomic situation. By viewing news and other English programs on television, we can improve our language skills, particularly in English. As a result, referring to it as an idiot box is inaccurate, as it is a box brimming with knowledge, amusement, and information. As a result, we should view it whenever we have free time and avoid being addicted to it.

Exercises

1.

Preference	Percentage
News	39%
Serials	18%
Sports	10%
Movies	7%
Music Channels	6%
Other Programme	20%
Total	100%

2.

Conveyance 30 %
Food & Fuel 10 %
Saving 7 %
Housemaid 10 %
Education 26 %
Clothing 17 %

3.

MUSICAL INSTRUMENTS
Wind
(Played by
blowing air)
Percussion
(Played by banging
and striking)
Stringed
(Played by moving
string)
Woodwind
Others
Harp
Guitar
Violin
Cello
Flute
Clarinet
Horn
Mouth Organ
Bagpipes

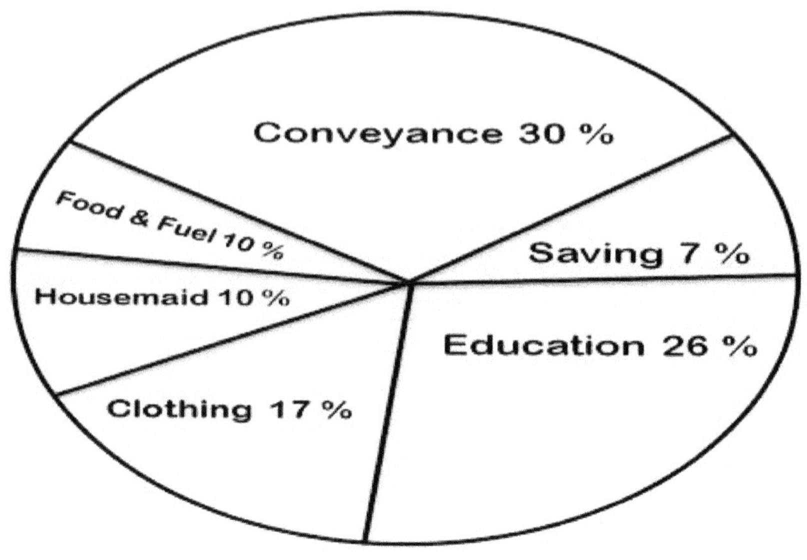

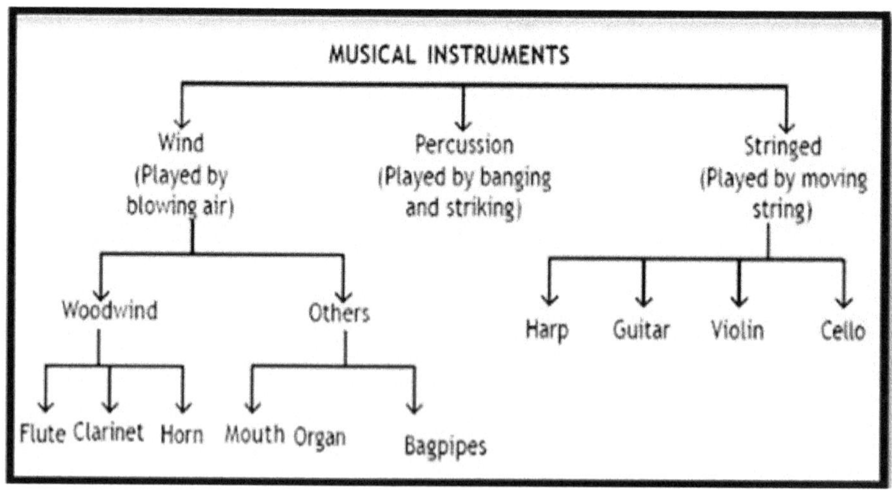

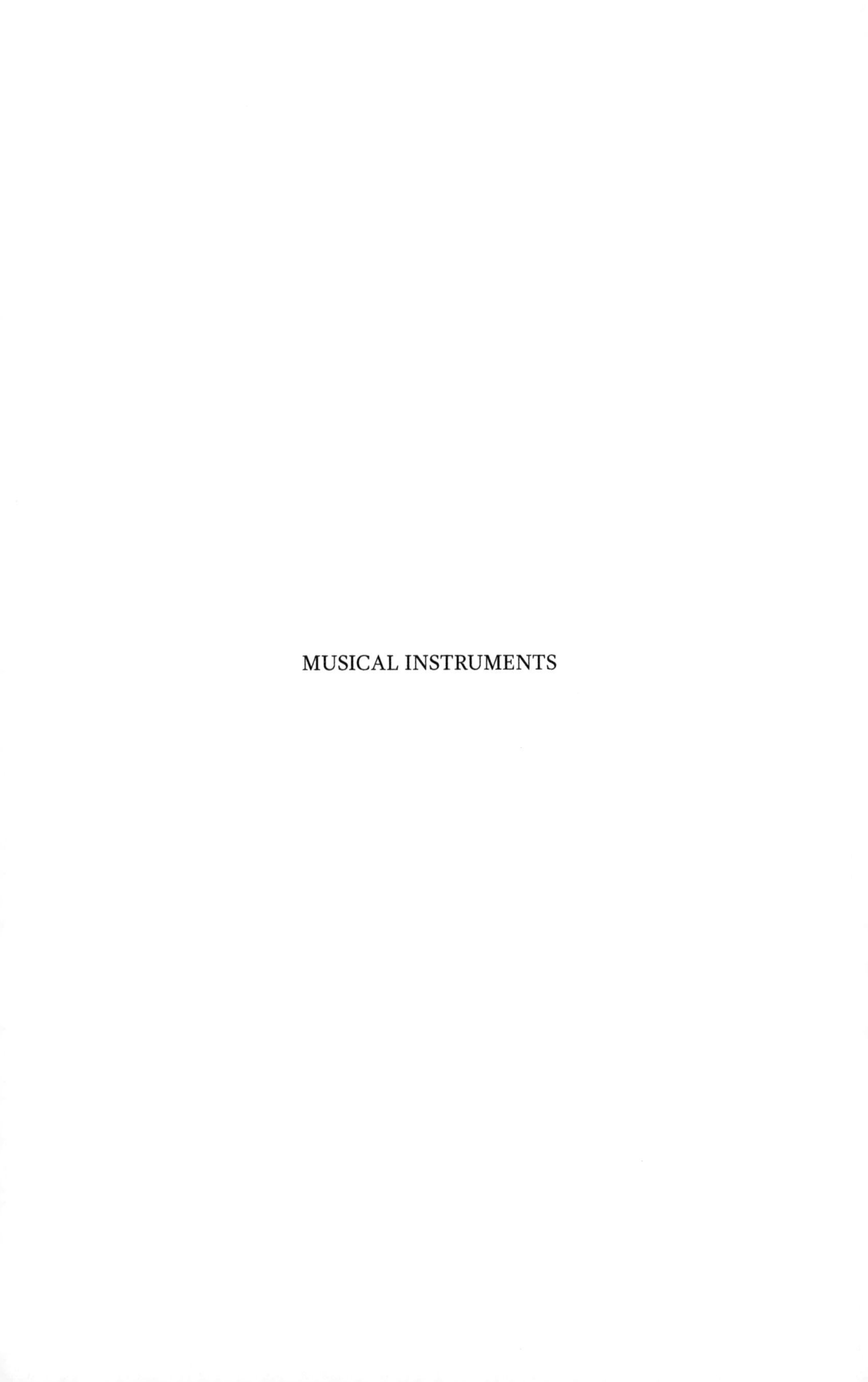

MUSICAL INSTRUMENTS

Report Writing

Reports might be scholarly, technical, or business-related, and they always include actionable recommendations. Reports are created to offer information regarding a scenario, project, or process, as well as to describe and assess the problem. A report's ultimate purpose is to communicate observations to a specific audience in a clear and succinct manner. Let's take a look at the right report writing format so you can create a polished final output.

A report is a brief document created for a specific audience or purpose. It usually outlines and analyses a problem, and it is frequently recommended for future use. The exact format of the report is determined by the department and organization

Newspaper or Magazine Reports:

The primary goal of a newspaper or magazine story is to cover a certain event or occurrence. They usually go over the 4Ws and 1H, which are What, Where, When, Why, and How. The following are the essential parts of producing a newspaper or magazine report:

Headline (Title)

Report's Name, Place, and Date

Body

Conclusion (Citation of sources)

Business reports

Business reports are intended to assess a scenario or case study using business theories and make recommendations for improvements. You must follow a formal writing style when producing a business report, and these reports are frequently longer than news stories because they try to examine a specific issue in depth and give answers. Business reports have the following fundamental structure:

- Table of Contents
- Executive summary
- Body
- Findings/Recommendations
- Conclusion

Technical Reports

The technical report's major goal is to give an empirical explanation of research-based content. A researcher writes technical reports for scientific publications, product development, and presentation, among other things. The majority of a technical report is comprised of

- Title Page
- Introduction
- Summary
- Experimental details
- Results and discussions
- Body (elaborating upon the findings)
- Conclusion

Report Writing:

A report is a written account of what you've witnessed, heard, done, or investigated. It is a logical and well-organized presentation of information and outcomes from a previously occurring event. Reports are a type of written assessment that is used to determine what you have learned through reading, study, or experience, as well as to provide you hands-on experience with a critical skill that is frequently utilized in the workplace.

Guidelines to write a Report

There are a few things you should consider when writing a report to ensure that you write an accurate and structured report, and they are given below:

i. Write a concise and clear title of the report.
v. Use the past tense whenever possible.
v. Don't talk about the problem in the first person, such as 'I' or 'Me.' write in the third person at all times.
v. After the heading, provide the date, the location's name, and the reporter's name.
v. Divide the report into paragraphs to make it easier to read.
v. Keep it descriptive and stick to the facts.
v. Use language that is unambiguous, concise and jargon-free.
v. Express facts and details in an unbiased manner.
v. Do not use slang or other informal words and contractions.
v. Organize the content for easy navigation and logical flow of information
v. Revise and proofread

Format of a Report

From

Date

To

Title of the report

Terms of Reference

Abstract/Summary

Body of the report

Conclusion

Signature

Sample Accident Report 1:

1.Suppose you are a manager of a company. Prepare a report on the fire that occurred at your workplace.

M.Rajesh,

The Floor Manager

27, Sholinganallur,

Lulu manufactures Pvt..Ltd.,

Madurai.

11/05/2022

To

The General Manager

Lulu Manufactures Pvt..LTd

Madurai.

Sir,

Sub: Report on the accident.

Ref: with reference to your memo no SS/BK/453 dated 3/04/2022,a detailed investigation has been made on 2/03/2022 in the factory premise

Workers were busy in the assembly line on March 2, 2022, and everything was going normally until a spark appeared in the area where a robot was welding. It spreads to the gunny bags that had been kept nearby. Workers on the floor utilized fire extinguishers to try to put out the fire as quickly as they could. Despite the prompt action, one individual passes out from asphyxia and is taken to the hospital.

During the examination, it was discovered that a short circuit had occurred in a portion of the robot that had been in service for about a year. As it was break time, the person in charge of the unit went to drink tea. Sudden oscillations in the power supply had resulted in a fire outbreak.

To prevent similar instances, it is suggested that:

- Careless personnel should be harshly reprimanded (The workers who had been careless should be punished severely);

- Machines should be maintained every other day;

- Power supply should be terminated automatically when there is an interruption; and

- Flammable goods such as gunny bags should be kept separately.

If such punitive and preventive measures are taken, such fire accident can be prevented in future.

Yours faithfully

(Signature)

M.Rajesh

Floor manager

2. Sample Report:

"Write a sample report on a fire accident due to leakage of electric current in a ladies hostel where two electrical engineering students died. Also give a set of recommendations for preventing such accidents in future". (May/June 2013)

To

The Principal

ABC Engineering College

Theni

Tamil Nadu

Date: 27th February 2022

Respected Sir,

Sub: Report on the fire accident

With reference to the accident that took place a couple of days ago in our college ladies hostel, the following report is submitted after a thorough analysis of the facts. Around 2:00 p.m. on February 25, 2022, a fire broke out in the female hostel. It was involved in a tragic fire disaster due to a power outage. It spread so swiftly that it devoured a broad area, devouring a large quantity of clothing and other goods stored in the Hostel. Because of the leak, the laundry room began to burn, and the fire spread to the upper floors. The students on the upper levels were studying for examinations, so everyone was confined to the room. Due to a large amount of smoke, several of the rooms were suffocated, but everyone in the building was warned and left safely. Furthermore, two female students on the top floor suffered burn injuries and were unable to leave the room.

The fire department was dispatched right away, and the two girls were protected from further harm. After an hour, the fire was put out. With significant burn injuries, the two female students were transferred to a neighbouring hospital. The doctors diagnosed and declared them as already dead. Furthermore, the doctor stated that they had asthma and that they died as a result of smoke and serious fire injuries.

Under investigations, it is found that the fire broke out because of a short circuit in the switch box. As all the fittings in the rooms were in operation, the fire chanced to spread very fast. This devastating fire accident has resulted in a loss of two girl students and a lakh of rupees.

Recommendations to prevent such mishaps

In order to avert or overcome such mishaps in future, the following precautions are recommended.

1. The worn out wiring should be immediately replaced and checked at regular intervals for leakages
2. It is extremely necessary to install more fire extinguishers at vantage points
3. Proper fuses must be installed to avoid the excess flow of current
4. Students should be trained to handle the electric components safely along with fire extinguishers
5. Fire alarms should be installed in Ladies Hostel, since a lot of students are available in the hostel.

If the above procedures are immediately implemented, such accidents can be avoided in the future, resulting in significant property and human damage.

Thank you,

Yours faithfully,

Sheela.M

Sample Survey Report:

As an Executive Director of an organization, conduct a national survey on oceans and their importance in the present scenario. Submit the report to the Chair person of your organization with detailed analysis and descriptions. Give certain recommendations to safe guard oceans and to give enlightenment for the society on oceans.

The Executive

Director Aquatics Control

Chennai-103

To

The Chair Person

Aquatics Control

Chennai-103

Sub: Report on Safeguarding Oceans

Ref: Your memo no. 123/54/22 dated on 12/03/2022 on safeguarding oceans

The public's relationships, values, attitudes, and knowledge of the oceans were investigated in a national telephone poll for The OCEAN Project. Our goal was to gain a better understanding of what has to be communicated in order to raise awareness and improve our concern for ocean health. Institute of Ocean Technology conducted six focus groups among people who had visited an aquarium, zoo, or science museum in the previous two years before embarking on the survey.

The focus group, which revealed critical values and beliefs while discussing ocean protection, considerably aided our knowledge of public opinions and the development of appropriate poll questions. The OCEAN

Project undertook a national survey of 1,500 adults in our society. From March 28 to June 29, a national survey of 1500 persons from our state answered dozens of questions about their feelings about the oceans. This section provides an overview and summary of the survey's important analytical points.

Aquariums, zoos, and science museums, as we discovered during the focus group part of this study, have a unique chance to teach the public about the importance of oceans. We are now unconcerned about the health of the seas, and we have discovered that the average population has only a rudimentary awareness of the oceans, their operations, and their importance to human survival. However, simply communicating information to the public will not likely improve the importance of these issues. We must combine factual information about the seas and the challenges they face with people's personal connections to the oceans, their values, and their daily lives in order to raise concern and urgency. Our examination of the poll data reveals significant insights into public perceptions of the seas, which will help aquariums, zoos, and science museums increase their commitment to ocean conservation.

When questioned about the health of the open, deep oceans, nearly half of the public says they don't know enough about them to make an informed decision, while slightly more than a quarter say the same about coastal waters. Americans who live within two hours of the ocean are more familiar with coastal seas, yet four out of ten have no opinion on the deep oceans. The preservation of the oceans is not a pressing concern. The oceans are not now considered to be in imminent danger, and the necessity for action to safeguard the oceans is not easily obvious.

Damage to the oceans is regarded a second-tier environmental hazard when we assess the severity of a number of environmental issues. Ocean threats are regarded as less dangerous than air and water pollution and toxic waste, but on par with global climate change, species extinction, and resource overconsumption in the state.

Recommendations

- It is suggested that every individual in the country be made aware of this situation.
- It is recommended that water from various businesses be recycled rather than polluting the oceans.
- When individuals use the ocean as a recreational area, it is recommended that they form a strong bond with it.
- Every person is asked to take seriously, the role of passing on information to the next generation in order to safeguard the oceans.
- To rescue those aquatics, it is recommended that fisheries and coastal organizations cease all hazardous practices in the water.

Exercises:

1. On the Jammu-Srinagar highway, a mishap took place, where a driver lost his control and skidded off in a deep gorge. Write a report on it and include all the necessary details and eyewitness accounts
2. Write today's trend of Covid 19 cases in India. As per the official statement. Include all the necessary details and factual information. Mention the state with a higher number of cases so far.

3. You are the technical representative of an engineering company. There is an issue in the manufacturing process of one of your products. Prepare a report analyzing the problem and making recommendations.

Reported Speech

Reported speech is how we represent other people's speech or what we say ourselves. Direct speech and indirect speech are the two basic categories of reported speech.

Direct speech repeats the exact words the person used, or how we remember their words:

Examples:

1. **Direct** : He said, "I want to go home".

Indirect : He said that he wanted to go home.

2. Direct : She said, "*I bought a gift* ***yesterday***."

Indirect : She said that she had bought a gift the previous day.

3. **Direct** : She said, "I am going to temple now".

Indirect : She said that she was going to temple then.

4. **Direct** : "*Where do they live?*"

Indirect : You asked me where they lived.

5. **Direct** : Raja said, "I can't work here".

Indirect : Raja said he couldn't work there.

When we look at the above sentence in indirect speech, we can see three different types of changes: Changes in pronouns, adverbs of time and place, and tenses

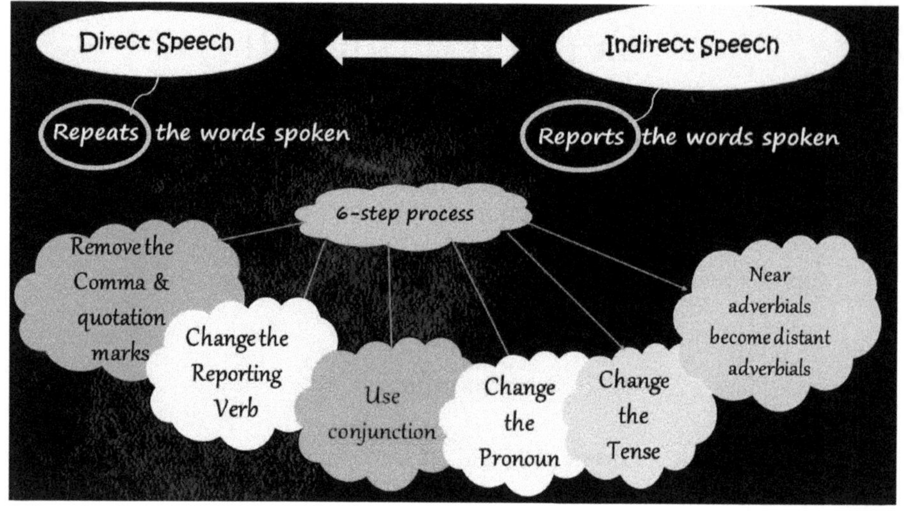

6 - STEP PROCESS

Pronoun change:

To learn the rules for changing pronoun, we should understand the two parts of the sentence. The first part of the sentence (he said, she said,) is called reporting verb. The second part of the sentence, which is enclosed in inverted commas, is called reported speech.

Direct : He said, "I complete the work".

Indirect : He said that he completed the work.

There are four easy rules for changing pronoun:

Rule 1: The pronoun of the reported speech is changed according to the pronoun (subject) of the reporting verb.

Eg: He said, "**I** will buy a dress"

He said that **he** would buy a dress.

Rule 2: If the reporting verb also carries a first person pronoun, the first person pronoun of reported speech is not modified.

Eg: I said, "**I** will buy a dress"

I said that I would buy a dress.

We said, "**We** saw a joker"

We said that **we** had seen a joker.

Rule 3: The second person pronoun of the reported speech is always changed according to the 'object pronoun' of the reporting verb.

Eg: He said to **me**, "**You** won a prize"

He said to me that **I** had won a prize.

Rule 4: The third person pronoun of the reported speech is not changed in indirect speech.

Eg: She said, "**He** works in a factory"

She said that **he** worked in a factory.

Change of Adverbs:

Phrase in direct speech Equivalent in reported speech

Today that day

"I saw him **today**", she said. She said that she had seen him **that day**.

Yesterday the day before

"I saw him **yesterday**", she said. She said that she had seen him **the day before.**

The day before yesterday two days before

"I met her **the day before yesterday**", he said. He said that he had met her **two days before.**

Tomorrow the next/following day

"I'll see you **tomorrow**", he said He said that he would see me **the next day**.

The day after tomorrow in two days time/ two days later

"We'll come **the day after tomorrow**", they said. They said that they would come **in two days time/ two days later. Next week/month/year the following week/month/year**

"I have an appointment **next week**", she said. She said that she had an appointment **the following week.**

Last week/month/year the previous/week/ month/year

"I was on holiday **last week**", he told us. He told us that he had been on holiday **the previous week.**

Ago Before

"I saw her **a week ago**," he said. He said he had seen her **a week before**.

this (for time) That

"I'm getting a new car **this week**", she said. She said she was getting a new car **that week.**

this/that (adjectives) The

"Do you like **this shirt**?" he asked He asked if I liked **the shirt**.

Here There

He said, "I live **here**". He told me he lived **there**.

Change of Tenses:

Tense Direct Speech Reported Speech

present simple I like ice cream She said (that) she liked ice cream.

present continuous I am living in London She said (that) she was living in London.

past simple I bought a car She said (that) she had bought a car

past continuous I was walking along the street She said (that) she had been walking along the street.

present perfect I haven't seen Julie She said (that) she hadn't seen Julie.

past perfect* I had taken English lessons before She said (that) she had taken English lessons before.

will I'll see you later She said (that) she would see me later.

would* I would help, but.." She said (that) she would help but...

Can I can speak perfect English She said (that) she could speak perfect English.

could* I could swim when I was four She said (that) she could swim when she was four.

Shall I shall come later She said (that) she would come later.

should* I should call my mother She said (that) she should call her mother.

might* I might be late She said (that) she might be late

must I must study at the weekend She said (that) she must study at the weekend

* **doesn't change.**

Note:

- If the reporting verb is in the simple present, present perfect or future there is no change of tense.

Eg: He says, "I will not take it".

He says that he will not take it.

- If the reported speech expresses a general truth, the tenses need not be changed.

Eg: Our teacher said, "The sun rises in the east".

Our teacher said that the sun rises in the east.

Reporting Statement:

Direct Speech	Indirect Speech
He said, 'I want to go.'	He said that he wanted to go.
Rakesh said, "I did the exam yesterday".	Rakesh said that he had done the exam the previous day.
He said, "I'm busy".	He said he was busy.
Meera said to Siva, "I'll help you".	Meera told Siva that she would help him. Meera promised to help Siva.

Reporting Questions:

1. **When we report questions, the subject comes before the verb**

Direct speech: "Where are you going?"
Reported speech: He asked me where I was going.

1. **We don't employ the auxiliary verb do when reporting queries, unless they're negative.**

Direct speech: "Who doesn't like cheese?"
Reported speech: She asked me who didn't like cheese.

3. **We report yes/no questions with *if* or *whether*.**

Direct speech: "Do you want me to come?"
Reported speech: I asked him if he wanted me to come.

4. **When we report questions with *who, what* or *which* + to be + object, the verb *be* can come before or after the object.**

Direct speech: "What is your favourite food?"
Reported speech: She asked me what my favourite food was / She asked me what was my favourite food.

<u>Reporting Commands / Imperative statements:</u>

Form

affirmative commands → to + infinitive

negative commands → not + to + infinitive

Affirmative commands

Direct Speech → Dad: "Do your homework."

Reported Speech → Dad told me to do my homework.

Negative commands

Direct Speech → Teacher: "Don't talk to your friend."

Reported Speech → The teacher told me not to talk to my friend.

Direct Speech Indirect Speech

Dad said, "Do your homework." Dad **told** me **todo** my homework.

He said, "Open the door". He ordered me to open the door

She said, "Don't be back late". She ordered me not to be back late.

He said to me "*Come with me*". *He* **told** *me* **to go** *with him.*

Reported Exclamation:

Depending on the nature of the exclamatory sentence in indirect speech, the words "exclaimed with joy," "exclaimed with grief," or "exclaimed with wonder" are added to the reporting verb.

Direct Speech Indirect Speech

He said, “Hurrah! I won a medal” He ***exclaimed with joy*** that he had won a medal.

She said, “Alas! I failed in exam” She ***exclaimed with sorrow*** that she failed in the exam.

Johnsi said, “Wow! What a nice skirt it is” Johnsi ***exclaimed with wonder*** that it was a nice skirt.

“How nice”, he exclaimed. She **exclaimed** that it was nice.

Problems of Must, Mustn’t, needn’t, let:

Direct Speech Indirect Speech

He said, "I must work tomorrow". He said he **had to [or must]** work the next day.

My sister said, “We **must** buy a new car”. My sister said that we **would have to** buy a new car.

She said to him, “You mustn’t go there”. She told her that **she mustn’t /wasn’t** to go there.

She told her **not to go** there. She said, “I needn’t wait for him”.

She said she needn't/didn't have to wait for him.

My friend said, "Let's watch TV". My friend suggested that we watch TV.

My friend suggested watching TV

Exercises

Change the following into Indirect Speech:

1. Raja said to Rani, "Are you going home today?"
2. He said, "The government must act on this!"
3. Raj said, "Where is she going?"
4. He said, 'I'll be driving the car myself once I have got my license.'
5. She said, 'My father died a week ago. I am yet to recover from the shock.'
6. My teacher often says to me, 'If you don't work hard, you will reach nowhere.'
7. Mother said John, 'I'll find a new job.'
8. She said, "Hurrah! I am selected for the job"
9. He says, "I am ill".
10. She said; "The exam is difficult".
11. She said, "I can speak perfect Spanish".
12. My father said, "Did you do your homework?
13. Michael said, "I may go there.'
14. I am reading a book, she explained.
15. She said, "I might come early."
16. Maria said to Raja, "Why are you going to school?"
17. He said, ""Have a seat."
18. She says, "I am a little bit nervous today."
19. He says, "I want to buy these books."
20. They said, "Madam, the time is over."
21. He *said* to me, "You should work hard to pass the exam."
22. He said to me, "Not to smoke."

23. We said to her, “Mind your own business”.
24. I said, “How lucky I am!”
25. You said to him, “What a beautiful drama you writing!

Answers:

1. Raja told rani that she was going home that day.
2. He said that the government would have to act on this."
3. Raj asked where she was going.
4. He said that he would be driving the car himself once he had got his license.
5. She said that her father had died a week ago and that she was yet to recover from the shock.
6. My teacher used to tell me that if I didn’t work hard I would reach nowhere.
7. John told his mother that he would find a new job.
8. She exclaimed with joy that she was selected for the job.
9. He says that he is ill.
10. She said that the exam was difficult.
11. She said that she could speak perfect Spanish.
12. My father asked me if I had done my homework.
13. Michael said that she might go there.
14. She explained that she was reading a book
15. She said she might come early.
16. Maria asked Raja why he was going to school.
17. He told me to have a seat.
18. She says that she is a little bit nervous that day.
19. He says that he wants to buy those books.
20. They said respectfully that the time was over.
21. He *advised* me that I should work hard to pass the exam.
22. He forbade me to smoke.
23. We urged her to mind her own business.
24. I said in great wonder that I was very lucky.
25. You said to him in great wonder that he was writing a beautiful drama.

Modals

Modal verbs are used to describe hypothetical conditions like guidance, capability, or requests. They're employed in conjunction with a main verb to somewhat alter its meaning. They can't always be employed on their own because they're auxiliary verbs. (A modal verb should only occur alone if the primary verb is obvious from the context.)

The main modals are as follows:

Shall, should, will, would, can, could, may, might, must, ought to, used to, need, dare, has/have/had to, etc.,

Modal verbs Modal verb usages Modal verb examples

Can Ability I can play the guitar very well.

Permission Can I sit now?

Possibility It can be a rainy day tomorrow.

Offer I can help you with this job. Don't worry!

Request Can you please pass me the water bottle?

Could Ability in the past I could play the guitar well when I was Ten.

Polite permission Excuse me, could I come in?

Possibility A hailstorm could come here at night.

Polite offer No problem. I could give you a help.

Polite request Could you please move to the next page?

May Permission May I leave early?

Possibility Scientists may discover a vaccine for corona virus.

Might Polite permission Might I take you home?

Possibility I might visit him evening if the weather is nice.

Must Obligation You must do the homework.

Certainly He must be at school now. He told me about that yesterday.

Mustn't Prohibition You mustn't play here. It's dangerous.

Will Prediction The weather forecast predicts that it will rain tomorrow.

Promise I will finish all the homework today.

Spontaneous decision I will lend you some cash.

Request/ demand Will you please give me that pen?

Would Used as the past form of "will" My dad said that he would give me some gifts on my birthday.

Polite request/ demand Would you mind closing the window, please?

Shall Prediction This time tomorrow I shall be in Japan.

Offer/ suggestion Shall we discuss this further with her?

Should Advice You should see the doctor. It's swollen.

Prediction/ expectation The project should be done this weekend.

Polite suggestion Should I call him to say sorry?

Ought to Obligation You ought to say good bye to your friends when you leave.

Advice You ought to sleep early. You look really tired.

Needn't talk about something not necessary You needn't give her any advice. She won't listen.

Exercises:

1. She ________ speak a little English.
2. ________ I go home, please?
3. When he was younger he ________ run fast.
4. ________ I call again on Wednesday?
5. I ______ take these books with me.
6. ________ you be available at 7 PM tonight?
7. You ________ have come to the meeting. It was interesting.
8. I ________ memorize all of the rules about discipline.
9. You ____________- smoke in this hotel. It's forbidden.
10. ______ I borrow your book?
11. Daniel ____ speak four languages.
12. ________ you recite it again more slowly?
13. You ____________ take off your slippers before you get into the temple.
14. You __________ do all the exercises, only the third one.
15. __________ you send the notebooks as soon as possible please?
16. She __________ make a decision about that shop before someone else buys it.
17. ________ I wear jeans to the office? – I'm afraid you may not because we have a strict dress code.
18. ________ my son play here?
19. She ___________ do the English homework so she asked her friend for help.
20. I think we _________ go at 6PM to avoid the rush-hour traffic.
21. You ___________ try this drink.

22. They _________ be at home yet. They only left three minutes ago!
23. He got four Ferraris. He __________- be very rich.
24. We __________- invite Raju and yuththika too.
25. Employees ________ not take the office equipment to home.
26. They _________ ride their motorcycles without helmets.
27. Marry _________ be home by now.
28. We ___________ go to the temple this weekend. It depends on the weather.
29. I think we __________ win this match but it'll be hard.
30. She __________ get tickets for the film because it was sold out.

Answers:

1. She **can** speak a little English.
2. **May** I go home, please?
3. When he was younger he **could** run fast.
4. **Shall** I call again on Wednesday?
5. I **will** take these books with me.
6. **Would** you be available at 7 PM tonight?
7. You **ought to** have come to the meeting. It was interesting.
8. I **must** memorize all of the rules about discipline.
9. You **mustn't** smoke in this hotel. It's forbidden.
10. **May** I borrow your book?
11. Daniel **can** speak four languages.
12. **Could** you recite it again more slowly?
13. You **have to** take off your slippers before you get into the temple.
14. You **don't have to** do all the exercises, only the third one.
15. **Would** you send the notebooks as soon as possible please?
16. She **ought to** make a decision about that shop before someone else buys it.
17. **May** I wear jeans to the office? – I'm afraid you may not because we have a strict dress code.
18. **Can** my son play here?
19. She **couldn't** do the English homework so she asked her friend for help.
20. I think we **should** go at 6PM to avoid the rush-hour traffic.

21. You **ought to** try this drink.
22. They **can't** be at home yet. They only left three minutes ago!
23. He got four Ferraris. He **must** be very rich.
24. We **should** invite Raju and yuththika too.
25. Employees **shall not** take the office equipment to home.
26. They **oughtn't** ride their motorcycles without helmets.
27. Marry **should** be home by now.
28. We **might** go to the temple this weekend. It depends on the weather.
29. I think we **could** win this match but it'll be hard.
30. She **couldn't** get tickets for the film because it was sold out.

Conjunctions

Conjunctions are words that connect two or more words, phrases, or clauses.

Eg: I enjoy cooking **and** eating, **but** I despise doing the dishes. Sophie is plainly fatigued, **yet** she insists on dancing till the wee hours of the morning.

Conjunctions allow you to construct complex, elegant statements without the choppiness that several short sentences might cause. Make sure the phrases that are connected by conjunctions are the same length (share the same structure).

Incorrect: I work quickly and careful.

Correct : I work quickly and carefully.

Types of Conjunctions:

There are 3 types of conjunctions

1. Coordinating conjunctions
2. Subordinating conjunctions
3. Correlative conjunctions

Coordinating Conjunctions:

Coordinating conjunctions unite words, phrases, and clauses in a sentence that have the same grammatical rank. The most common coordinating conjunctions are for, and, nor, but, or, yet, and so; the mnemonic device FANBOYS can help you recall them.

Eg: He invited me, **but** I didn't go.

We can play football **or** basketball.

Notice the use of the comma when a coordinating conjunction is joining two independent clauses.

Subordinating Conjunctions:

Independent and dependent clauses are joined by subordinating conjunctions. A subordinating conjunction can indicate a cause-and-effect relationship, a contrast, or any other relationship between sentences.

The most common subordinating conjunctions include:

after, although, as, as if, as long as, as much as, as soon as, as though, because, before, by the time, even if, even though, if, in order that, in case, in the event that, lest , now that, once, only, only if, provided that, since, so, supposing, that, than, though, till, unless, until, when, whenever, where, whereas, wherever, whether or not, while

Eg: He can stay out until the clock strikes ten.

She didn't go to the office because she was ill.

Here, the adverb until functions as a subordinating conjunction to connect two ideas: He can stay out (the independent clause) and the clock strikes ten (the dependent clause). The independent clause could stand alone as a sentence; the dependent clause depends on the independent clause to make sense.

Correlative conjunctions

Correlative conjunctions work in pairs to join words and groups of words of equal weight in a sentence. There are many different pairs of correlative conjunctions:

either...or both...and

not only...but (also) whether...or

neither...nor just as...so

the...the rather...than

as...as not...but rather

as much...as Not so...as

no sooner...than In order that

Conjunctions of time:

Examples:

After - We'll do the work *after* you do this.

as long as - That's fine *as long as* he agrees to our conditions.

as soon as - We'll get to that *as soon as* we finish this.

by the time - She had left *by the time* you arrived.

long before - We'll be gone *long before* you arrive.

now that - We can get going *now that* they have left.

Once - We'll have less to worry about *once* the boss leaves.

since - We haven't been able to upload our work *since* the network went down.

Till - Please hold on *till* the guest entry.

until - We are waiting *until* you send us the confirmation.

when - She can do what she wants *when* she wants.

whenever - There is a good chance of rain *whenever* there are clouds in the sky.

while - I really appreciate you waiting *while* I finish up.

Exercises:

1. The teacher was frustrated, ______ the school had cut funding for all enrichment programs
2. The patient complained of back pain, ____she refused treatment.
3. Both the students _____ the teachers were satisfied with the annual program.
4. Students who did not complete the project received _______ prize ___ awards.
5. The teacher gave the test ________ delivering the instructions.
6. The author must avoid prejudice ___ she wants to maintain an academic tone.
7. The flower is rose, ______ it has a particular smell.
8. He proudly showed me the award _______ he bought yesterday.
9. The talented acrobats impressed _____ the children _____ their parents.
10. ___________ It rains, we stay inside _____watch movies.
11. I need shirts that are __________ red ___ pink.
12. I am hungry _______- tired
13. He tried to buy some clothes, ______ the store was closed
14. I'll eat pista, chocolate, ___ strawberry ice cream.
15. I passed the test _________ I studied hard.
16. I'd like to thank you _______ the lovely party.
17. I want to go for a party ________ I have to go to work today.
18. They do not smoke, nor do they play cards.
19. I have three dogs ___ a cat.
20. To be, ____ not to be?
21. He eats at the café every Sunday, ____ they serve the best bagels in town.
22. Would you rather wear a saree ___ jeans?
23. I don't like vegetables, _______ I think ragi and wheat are delicious.
24. _________ of my dad, I know how to play Volleyball.

25. I can't go to bed _______ I brush my teeth.
26. The postman delivered a package ______ you were at school.
27. You can eat a banana ______ you get hungry before breakfast.
28. I can't decide ____________ I want ice or chocolates.
29. She has been working in this company ________ 1989.
30. Let me check ________ he's in her room.
31. I loved to play outdoor games _______ I was a kid
32. You're going to attend English class, _____ you like it _______ not.
33. I want to visit ______ Dubai ___ Singapore.
34. I want to be ___________ a wife and mother, _______ a Teacher.
35. He is very funny________ she is boring.

Answers:

1. The teacher was frustrated, **for** the school had cut funding for all enrichment programs
2. The patient complained of back pain, **yet** she refused treatment.
3. Both the students **and** the teachers were satisfied with the annual program.
4. Students who did not complete the project received **neither** prize **nor** awards.
5. The teacher gave the test **after** delivering the instructions.
6. The author must avoid prejudice **if** she wants to maintain an academic tone.
7. The flower is rose, **and** it has a particular smell.
8. He proudly showed me the award **that** he bought yesterday.
9. The talented acrobats impressed **both** the children **and** their parents.
10. **Whenever** it rains, we stay inside **and** watch movies.
11. I need shirts that are **either** red **or** pink.
12. I am hungry **and** tired
13. He tried to buy some clothes, **but** the store was closed
14. I'll eat pista, chocolate, **or** strawberry ice cream.
15. I passed the test **because** I studied hard.
16. I'd like to thank you **for** the lovely party.
17. I want to go for a party **but** I have to go to work today.

18. They do not smoke, nor do they play cards.
19. I have three dogs **and** a cat.
20. To be, **or** not to be?
21. He eats at the café every Sunday, **for** they serve the best bagels in town.
22. Would you rather wear a saree **or** jeans?
23. I don't like vegetables, **yet** I think ragi and wheat are delicious.
24. **Because** of my dad, I know how to play Volleyball.
25. I can't go to bed **until** I brush my teeth.
26. The postman delivered a package **while** you were at school.
27. You can eat a banana **if** you get hungry before breakfast.
28. I can't decide **whether** I want ice or chocolates.
29. She has been working in this company **since** 1989.
30. Let me check **whether** he's in her room.
31. I loved to play outdoor games **when** I was a kid
32. You're going to attend English class, **whether** you like it **or** not.
33. I want to visit **either** Dubai **or** Singapore.
34. I want to be **not only** a wife and mother, **but also** a Teacher.
35. He is very funny **whereas** she is boring.

Prepositions

A preposition is a word or set of words that comes before a noun, pronoun, or noun phrase to indicate direction, time, place, location, spatial relationships, or to introduce an object. Words like "in," "at," "on," "of," and "to" are examples of prepositions.

In English, prepositions are quite idiomatic. Although there are some usage guidelines, fixed expressions govern a lot of preposition usage. It is preferable to memorize the phrase rather than the individual preposition in these situations.

There are over 100 prepositions in English. The most common single-word prepositions are:

About, beside, near, to, above, between, of, towards, across, beyond, off, under, after, by, on, underneath, against, despite, onto, unlike, along, down, opposite, until, among, during, out, up, around, except, outside, upon, as, for, over, via, at, from, past, with, before, in, round, within, behind, inside, since, without, below, into, than, beneath, like, through,

Although most prepositions are single words, some pairs and groups of words operate like single prepositions:

The most common prepositions that consist of groups of words are:

ahead of, except for, instead of, owing to, apart from, in addition to, near to, such as, as for, in front of, on account of, thanks to, as well as, in place of, on top of, up to, because of, in spite of, out of, due to, inside of, outside of,

Prepositions of Direction	to, in, into, on and onto.	She drove to the home.
Prepositions of Time	in, at and on.	He was born in 1888.
Prepositions of Place	"in" (the point itself), "at" (the general vicinity), "on" (the surface), and "inside" (something contained).	He left his phone on the sofa.
Prepositions of Location	"in" (an area or volume), "at" (a point), and "on" (a surface).	He will find her at the Classroom.
Prepositions of Spatial Relationships	above, across, against, ahead of, along, among, around, behind, below, beneath,beside,between, from, in front of, inside, near, off, out of, through, toward, under, and within.	The kids are hiding behind the house.

Exercises:

1. They weren't aware _____ COVID.
2. Is Urdu very different _____ Hindi?
3. This picture is similar __ the one in our Drawing room.
4. What's wrong ______ Ravi?
5. We were really surprised ___ the price of Chicken fried rice in restaurants on our holiday.
6. Exercise is good __ everyone.
7. Does anyone know the cause __ the disease?
8. _____which room are they having dinner?

9. Have you bought ____ your father?
10. I should rewrite the conclusion __ my essay.
11. Sanjai left his wallet _____ the car.
12. We're cooking _____ twelve guests tonight.
13. The bird flew _______ the tree.
14. She worried ________ the future.
15. She suffers ________ Malaria.
16. The same problem occurred _____ two out of five cases.
17. She argued _________ her mother.
18. He is not crazy ________ Chinese food.
19. The children are busy _______ their homework.
20. He is famous _____ his glass paintings.
21. We will meet _____ breakfast.
22. A new bridge is ______ construction.
23. She described the project _______ detail.
24. She's ___ leave until the end of the month.
25. We stayed at home ________ the conference.
26. She left the shop ______ an hour ago.
27. We should send a reply _________seven days.
28. She ran _______- him with the book.
29. Are you happy _______ that arrangement?
30. I feel very proud _____be a part of the team.

Answers:

1. They weren't **awareof** COVID.
2. Is Urdu very different **from** Hindi?
3. This picture is **similar to** the one in our Drawing room.
4. What's **wrong with** Ravi?
5. We were really surprised **at** the price of Chicken fried rice in restaurants on our holiday.
6. Exercise is **good for** everyone.
7. Does anyone know the cause **of** the disease?
8. **In which** room are they having dinner?
9. Have you bought **from** your father?

10. I should rewrite the conclusion **of** my essay.
11. Sanjai left his wallet **in** the car.
12. We're cooking **for** twelve guests tonight.
13. The bird flew **over** the tree.
14. She worried **about** the future.
15. She suffers **from** Malaria.
16. The same problem occurred **in** two out of five cases.
17. She argued **with** her mother.
18. He is not crazy **about** Chinese food.
19. The children are busy **with** their homework.
20. He is famous **for** his glass paintings.
21. We will meet **after** breakfast.
22. A new bridge is **under** construction.
23. She described the project **in** detail.
24. She's **on** leave until the end of the month.
25. We stayed at home **during** the conference.
26. She left the shop over an hour **ago.**
27. We should send a reply **within** seven days.
28. She ran **after** him with the book.
29. Are you happy **with** that arrangement?
30. I feel very proud **to** be a part of the team.

CHAPTER FIVE

UNIT V: THE ABILITY TO PUT IDEAS OR INFORMATION COGENTLY JOB APPLICATION

A cover letter is one of the most effective ways to communicate why you are the greatest candidate for the internship. As a result, you'll be able to expand on and highlight relevant talents and experiences.

A well-written cover letter should highlight important abilities and experiences that qualify you for the position. It should also pique (capture) the employer's interest and persuade them to read your CV in detail. A few details should be included in the cover letter to achieve these objectives.

- Specify the position for which you're applying.
- Use the appropriate keywords.
- Include any coursework that is relevant.
- Make a point to emphasize relevant abilities.
- Justify why you're the best candidate for the internship.
- Describe how you believe the internship will benefit you.
- Before you send your cover letter, double-check it.

Cover Letter Template for Internships

1. **Your contact information**, including at least your phone and email.
2. **Date of writing.**
3. **The hiring manager's contact information**, including company name and address.
4. **Salutation** (or greeting) — *Dear Hiring Manager* or *Dear* + hiring manager's surname will work perfectly fine.
5. **First paragraph** — hook the reader with a strong, engaging introduction.
6. **Second paragraph** — expand on why you're the perfect candidate, focusing on your measurable achievements and relevant skills.
7. **Third paragraph** — explain why you want this job more than any other.
8. **Final paragraph** — your closing statements, including a call to action.
9. **Sign-off** — *Best regards,* followed by your full name.

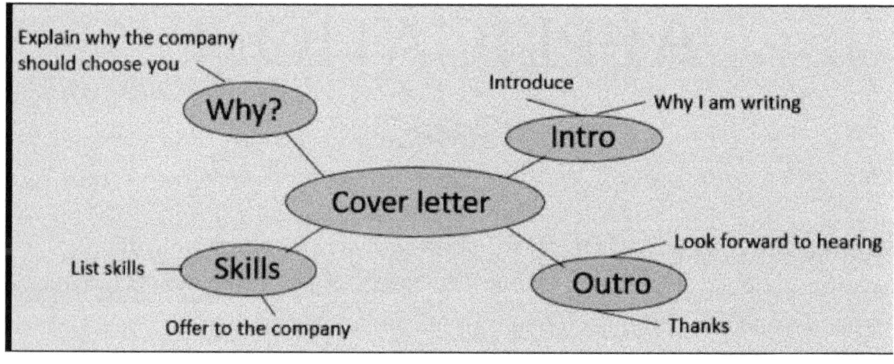

Cover Letter

Paragraph 1

First, provide a formal introduction and mention how you learned about the internship. Include some background information and a statement about why you're applying.

Paragraph 2

Abilities and achievements added to your resume in the second paragraph. Include instances of times when you've excelled in a professional or academic position, as well as your enthusiasm for the sector. Focus on your academic credentials if you're writing an internship cover letter for the first time.

Paragraph 3

Here you can explain anything that makes your application unique. Do some research on the firm and explain why you think you'd be a good fit for its culture. Or, explain why you want to work there because of its good impact on your town (or society at large).

Paragraph 4

A call to action should be included at the conclusion of your application. Thank the reader for their time and tell them you're ready to be interviewed. Finally, sign off with "Sincerely," followed by your name.

Sample Internship Cover Letter 1(Internship in Marketing)

To

Dr.Rajesh Sharma

Human Resources Manager,

Employment Avenue,

Chennai.

Dear Sir/Madam

I noticed your advertising on the ABC College employment board soliciting applications for a marketing internship at Brand Solutions Inc. with great interest.

As a marketing student, I've completed upper-division coursework in marketing management, print and online advertising, social media management, and data analysis, all of which have given me a good grasp on emerging market strategies and technology. On-site practicum (workshop, seminar) with Boyd Brothers LLC and Boulevard Bistro were part of this program, and I assisted the proprietors of these companies in establishing their first-ever social media presence on Facebook, LinkedIn, Instagram, and Twitter. This included creating accounts, developing photo and video material, writing posts, starting digital ad campaigns, and using Google Analytics and Facebook Analytics to analyze user engagement. I also know how to utilize Adobe Creative Cloud and Microsoft Office Suite for graphic design.

I'm excited about the challenges and opportunities I'll have as your next marketing intern, after reading about Brand Solutions Inc. in Market Branding Today and on Forbes Online. I've included my resume; could we perhaps set up a personal interview to go through my qualifications for this position in greater depth? Thank you for your thought, time, and prompt answer.

Sincerely

M.Santhosh

Sample Internship Cover Letter 1(Design internship program)

To

R.Ramkumar

XXXX(company name)

Madurai.

Dear Sir/Madam

I'm submitting my résumé to ABC Company for consideration as a summer application design internship program. I believe I will be a valuable contributor to your team, based on the skills and experience listed in my accompanying resume.

I've completed a lot of coursework on cutting-edge design trends and best practices at XYZ College, including Principles of User Experience Design and Mobile Application Design, where I learned and applied skills like user journey mapping, application wire framing, and designing software for a variety of mobile devices and operating systems.

In addition, I spent the previous semester volunteering with a local non-profit that collects donated clothing and delivers it to the families in need. I assisted the web team in updating and re-launching an app that allows residents to find nearby drop-off points and schedule pick-ups.

Volunteering with the non-profit has also taught me the value of creating a user-friendly and memorable brand experience. It also aided in the development of my teamwork, verbal communication, and project management abilities.

I believe I would be a valuable member of your team. This internship would allow me to gain valuable real-world experience in the technology industry while also allowing me to improve and enhance my application design abilities.

I eagerly await your response!

Sincerely,

XXXX(Name).

Key Takeaways

Now, let's do a small recap of the key learning points we just covered:

- Cover letters are a must when you're applying for an internship.
- When you start writing your cover letter, make sure you respect the format: the header with contact information, the greeting to the recruiter, an opening paragraph, the body with 2-3 paragraphs, and a closing paragraph followed by an official salutation and your name.
- Some of our main tips on how to write a cover letter for an internship include: state the position you're applying for, make use of the right keywords, and back up your skills with experiences.
- Use a cover letter builder and match it with your resume to make sure your cover letter truly stands out from the rest.

Cover Letter / Resume

A job application letter is simply a lengthy pitch designed to persuade a potential employer that you are qualified for the position for which you are applying. The letter will showcase your qualifications, skills, experience, and achievements in addition to expressing your interest in the job. It will demonstrate why you are the ideal candidate for the job and persuade the recruiter to invite you for an interview. Overall, a well-written application will paint a positive picture of you as a person and a professional, and employers will be impressed.

Follow these steps to write a letter:

i. Read the job description carefully.
v. Review letter formats used in the professional world.
v. Make a distinct heading for your paragraph.
v. Describe your qualifications for the position.
v. Your attributes should be highlighted.
v. Conclude the letter with Thank you.

Template for job application letter

It would be easy to draught a new job application letter if you use this job application letter template.

To: Company address

Subject: Application for XYZ position at ABC company

Message Body:

Salutation (Dear/Hello Sir/Madam/Mr./Mrs./Ms.)

Begin by mentioning the job opening and where you found it, expressing your interest in it, and providing a brief introduction of yourself and your professional title.

Highlight your educational qualifications, your professional skills and your work experience to emphasize your suitability for the job position.

Provide details of your previous work projects with other companies and explain how these improve your ability to meet and exceed the employer's expectations.

Thank the recruiter or hiring manager for reading the letter.

Sincerely/Best Regards

Your name

Mobile number

Email

Example 1:

Software Developer Application Letter:

Plot no.42, Mullai street,

Madurai

28 October 2022

To

The Manager

Cisco Private Limited

Hyderabad

This is regarding your post on {Portal} about a vacancy in your company for the role of Software Developer. Kindly find my resume here with.

Here is a brief about myself. I have completed B.Tech in Computer Science from {Institute Name}. I secured {Marks/Grade} in my final exams and passed with {distinction/Percentage}.

During my studies, I participated in various tech fests and also won a gold medal for creating an app from scratch in an inter-university tech competition.

I am confident that I have the skills to excel at your dynamic organization. I have always dreamed of being a part of your company due to the development opportunities you provide. I request you to give me an opportunity to learn and grow at your esteemed firm through this job role.

Kindly refer to my resume and cover letter, attached with the email, for detailed information.

Thank You.

Yours sincerely,

{Your Name}

Mobile:{Your Contact Number}

Email Id:{Your Email Address)

Example 2:

Sales Manager Application Letter:

Plot no.42, Mullai street,

Madurai

28 October 2022

To

The Manager

Cisco Private Limited

Hyderabad

Subject: Application for Sales Manager

Dear Mr. Acharya

This is in response to your advertisement for a sales manager in The Hindu dated on 27/10/22. I've read the job criteria and looked at the Cisco Private Limited website, and I would like to work for you.

I hold a first-class MBA from Symbiosis and have worked as a Marketing Manager at Aajivan Biscuits for the past seven years. Ideating, planning, and organising product launches and customer interaction campaigns are among my professional accomplishments. We were able to achieve increased sales five years in a row as a result of these efforts. I believe I will be a good fit for the role in your organisation because of my knowledge and enthusiasm for marketing techniques.

Please see my attached resume and work samples.

Thank you for taking the time to consider my application.

I hope to hear from you.

Best regards,

M.Balamurugan

+91 98765 43210

bala@abcmail.com

Example 3:

Project Manager Application letter

46, R.V.Nagar,

Chennai

Date: 21/04/22

To

The Manager

TCS Private Ltd.,

Chennai

Subject: Application for the Post of {Project Manager}

Dear Mr./Ms./Mrs. {Recipient's Name},

I am writing in response to your advertisement in The Hindu for the post of Project Manager's role at your firm. I would like to apply for the same.

As a Project Manager my track record of completing every project within the given time and budget proves my efficiency. I have worked extensively in the social sector as well as with corporate organizations.

My skills match your requirements well, and I have attached my detailed profile to this email for your consideration.

I hope to discuss this opportunity with you in person. Thank you for considering my application.

Yours sincerely,

{Your Name}

Mob: {Your Contact Number}

Email Id: {Your Email Address)

Resume Sample 1(for fresher)

Rajesh Sharma

170 RS Road, Gandhi Nagar,

Coimbatore.

Career Objective

To work for an organization that allows me to develop my skills and knowledge in order to help the company achieve its goals.

Profile summary

An enthusiastic fresher with highly motivated and leadership skills having bachelors of engineering degree in Mechanical Engineering..

I'm always looking for new technologies and approaches to learn.

Looking for new methods to improve technology.

Academic Qualification:

Examination	School/college	Board/University	Year	Result
B.E.,	ABC College	Anna university	XXXX	87%
Higher Secondary	ASW School	CBSE	XXXX	73%
High School	MSS School	CBSE	XXXX	90%

Achievements

- TVS awarded me FOUR suggestion certificates for my top ideas.
- "SAE INDIA MEMBER" and attended an SAEINDIA one-day session.
- Participated in the International Conference on Energy and Environmental Emerging Trends.
- Basic Life Support and First Aid Skills training have been completed.
- Basic Fire Safety and Emergency Preparedness training has been completed.
- Awarded by College for securing second rank in the University Examinations.
- The year's Best Exiting Student Award.

Individual Skills Sets

- High energy and a desire to learn new things.
- Strong leadership and motivational abilities.
- Ability to generate the finest results under stress.
- Excellent written and verbal communication abilities.
- Ability to operate independently as well as in a team.

Technical Qualification

- 2D Drafting Package: AutoCAD.
- 3D Drafting Package: Solid Edge
- Analysis Package: Femap

Experience

Summer Internship

Trained in all aspects of customer care

Personal Details

Languages Known- Hindi, English

DOB- MM/DD/YYYY

Address- NBJSBJSB

Resume Sample 2

Ashish XXXXXXX

Mobile No:- 9xxxxxxxx
Email: ashuxxxxxx@yahoo.co.in

CAREER STATEMENT

IT Professional seeking a challenging and rewarding opportunity with an organization of repute which recognizes and utilizes my true potential while nurturing my analytical and technical skills in the field of IT.

EDUCATIONAL QUALIFICATIONS

2012: B.Tech from XXXXXXX College of Engineering & Technology
Percentage: 67.40%

2008: 12th from XXXXX College (XXXXX Board) with XX % marks

2006: 10th from XXXXX College (XXXXX Board) with XX % marks

COMPUTER KNOWLEDGE

Languages: C, C++ and ASP with C# (.Net Platform).
Platforms: Windows 7, Windows Vista and Windows XP.

INDUSTRIAL EXPOSURE

Company: XXXXXX
Designation: Summer Trainee
Duration: XXXX-XXXX
Roles & responsibilities

- Understanding the needs of customers and offering them superior products and service
- Building long lasting relationships with their partners.

INTERESTS

- Programming
- Listening Music.

AWARDS AND ACHIEVEMENTS

- Participated in inter – collegiate competition.
- Gold Club Membership by ICICI PRU.

EXTRA CURRICULER ACTIVITIES

- President, Student association
- Volunteer, National Social Service
- Member, Rotract Club

PERSONAL DETAILS

Date of Birth: XXXX
Languages known: XXXXX
Permanent Address: XXXXX

Exercise:

1. Write an application with an enclosed resume for the post of Electrical Engineer in a company highlighting your skills and experience.
2. Wanted a Manager at our new factory in Delhi. Engineering with minimum 3 years experience in manufacturing industries as manager can apply. Apply with particulars to plot no.28, The Hindu, Chennai -6000014.
3. You are MBA in marketing with an Engineering graduate. Draft a covering letter and a resume for the position of manager in an

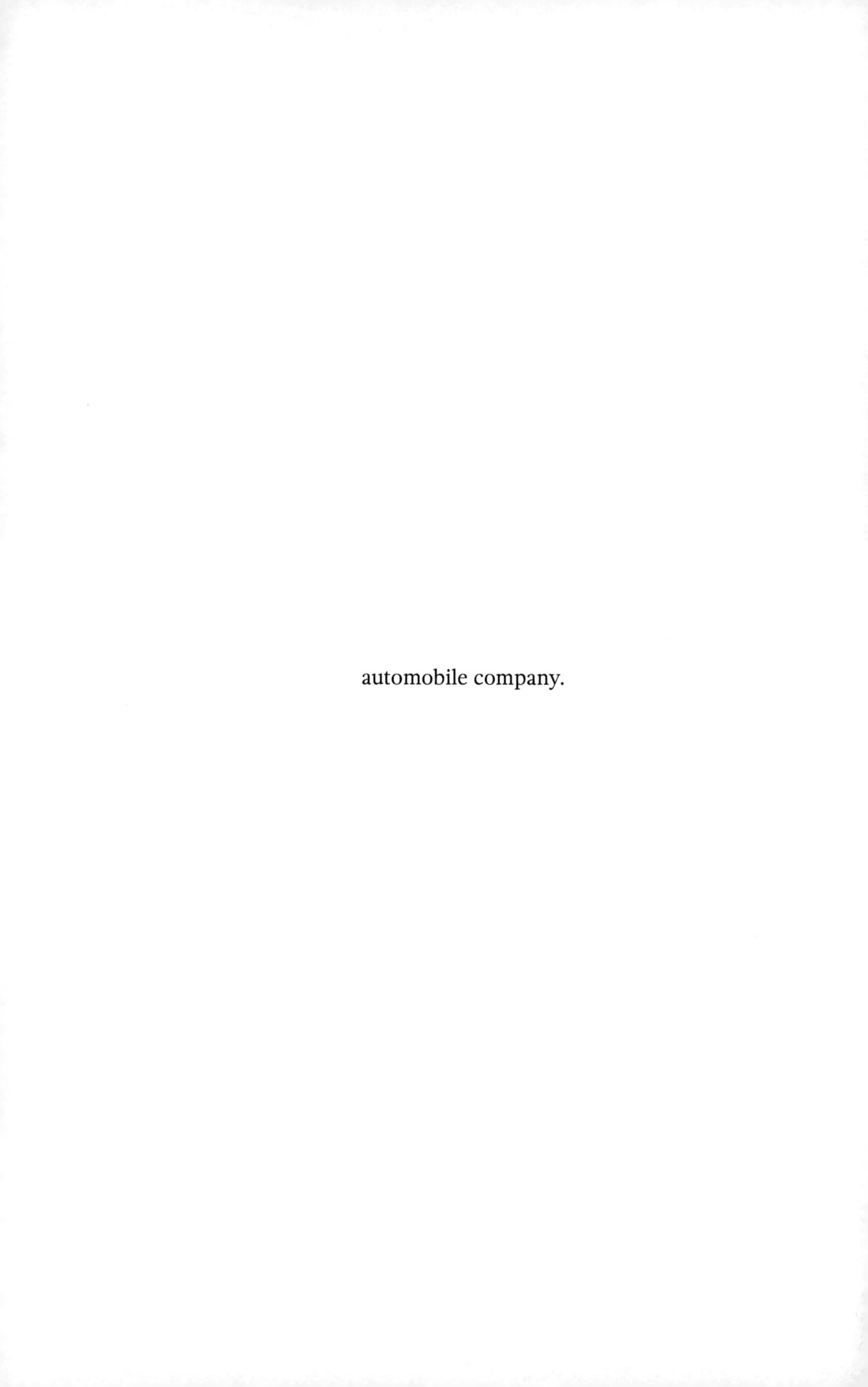

automobile company.

Numerical Adjectives

The numeral adjective is also called the adjective of numbers. It is used in a sentence to represent the numbers or order of any material or anything else. It delivers additional details and correct information in a sentence as a result of the number sequences.

Sometimes, a quantitative adjective also functions as a numeral adjective

Types of Numeral Adjectives

There are three types of numeral adjectives. These three categories are used to represent number adjectives in various scenarios.

Definite numeral adjective

Indefinite numeral adjective and

Distributive numeral adjective.

Definite Numeral Adjectives (cardinal and ordinal)

Numerical adjectives are those that express numbers or numerical adjective is simply the grammatical term for numbers. They include one, two, three, first, second, and many others.

Numerical adjectives are divided into:

Cardinal Adjectives: It shows how many. It is used for counting.

Examples: One life, five apples.

Ordinal Adjectives: It shows which one of a series. It is used for ranking.

Examples: The third floor, The first chapter

Indefinite numeral adjective

When you witness words like some, few, many, all, certain, several in a sentence then this is an indefinite adjective.

Eg: She has bought **all** the tomatoes.

3. **Distributive Numeral Adjective**: In a sentence when the words such as each, every, neither, either are used to describe then it is known as a distributive numeral adjective.

Eg: **Every** student needs job.

Expand the following:

5000rev/min Five thousand revolutions per minute

150 rpm One hundred and fifty revolutions per minute

400ppm Four hundred parts per million

6,28m/s Six point two eight metres per second

40%w/v Forty percentage weight per volume

530 kHz Five hundred and thirty kilohertz

1500kg/cm3 One thousand five hundred kilogram per centimeter cube

273K Two hundred and seventy three Kelvin

500Btu/ft3 Five hundred British thermal units per cubic feet.

15 psi Fifteen pounds per square inch.

40 ppm Forty parts per million

NUMERICAL ADJECTIVES

Rewrite the following as numerical adjectives:

Note: When the numerical expression is placed in the position of an adjective before the noun, the single form of the number is used. The plural form is not used.

Examples:

1. A journey of 20 miles: **A 20-mile journey.**

2. A project of 10 years: **A 10-year project.**

3. A vocation for thirty days: **A 30-day vocation**

4. A workshop for 5 days: **A five- day workshop.**

5. A walk of 5 kilometers: **A five- kilometer walk.**

6. A tank with a capacity of 1000 litres: **A 1000-litre (capacity) tank**

7. A research grant of Rs.2 lakhs: **A two- lakh rupee research grant.**

8, A lamp of a power of 60 watts **A 60- watt lamp**

9. A match lasting for 5 days: **A five day match**

10. A flask with a capacity of 2 litres: A **two- litre flask**

11. A squad of 1000 men: **A 1000-.man squad**

12. An interval of 10 minutes: **A ten- minute interval**

13. A DC supply of 240 volts: **A 240- watt DC supply**

14. A team consisting of 3 men: **A three- man team.**

15. A book with 80 pages: **A 80-page book**

16. A group of 10 nations: **A ten- nation group**

17. A college that is 40 years old: **A forty-year old college.**

18. A highway of 456 kilometres: **A 456- kilometer highway**

19. A workforce of 300 men: **A 300- man work force.**

20. A seminar held for two days: **A two-day seminar.**

21. a building with six floors: **A six –floor building**

22. An industry that is 20 years old: **A 20-year old industry.**

23. A bottle containing 2 litres of water: **A two- litre water bottle.**

24. An expedition lasting for three days: **A three- day expedition**

25.A project proposal for 10 crores: **A ten- crore project proposal**

Exercise:

Rewrite the following as numerical adjectives (Anna university April/ May 2018)

1. Three barrels which can hold five litres each

2. Storage space of 32 giga bytes

3. An electric cable which is ten metres length

4. Project lasting for two years

Check your answers:

1. A five- litre three barrels.

2. A 32- giga byte storage space

3. A ten- metre electric cable

4. A two- year project.

Relative Clauses

Relative clauses can be used to connect two English sentences or to provide additional information.

I bought a new bike. It is very costly.
→ **I bought a new bike that is very costly.**

She lives in India. She likes living in India.
→ **She lives in India, which she likes.**

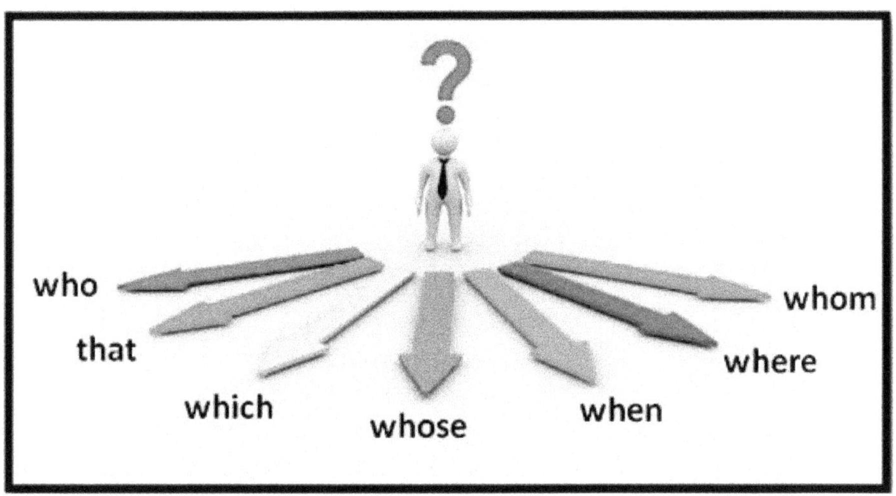

RELATIVE CLAUSES

Types: Defining and Non-defining

A **defining relative clause** tells which noun we are talking about:

- I like the man who lives next door.

(If I don't say 'who lives next door', then we don't know which man I mean).

A **non-defining relative clause** gives us extra information about something. We don't need this information to understand the sentence.

- I live in London, which has some fantastic parks.

(Everybody knows where London is, so 'which has some fantastic parks' is extra information).

Defining relative clauses:

1: The relative pronoun is the subject:

First, let's consider when the relative pronoun is the subject of a defining relative clause.We can use 'who', 'which' or 'that'. We use

- 'who' for people and
- 'which' for things
- 'that' for people or things.

The relative clause can come after the subject or the object of the sentence. We can't drop the relative pronoun.

For example (clause after the object of the sentence):

- I'm looking for a student who / that can use a computer well.
- She has a daughter who / that is a doctor.
- He bought a house which / that is 100 years old.
- I sent a letter which / that arrived two weeks later.

More examples (clause after the subject of the sentence):

- The people who / that live on the island are very friendly.
- The woman who / that phoned is my sister.
- The camera which / that costs Rs.1000 is over there.
- The house which / that belongs to sheela is in Chennai

2: The relative pronoun is the object:

Next, let's talk about when the relative pronoun is the object of the clause. In this case we can drop the relative pronoun if we want to. Again, the clause can come after the subject or the object of the sentence. Here are some examples:

(Clause after the object)

- She loves the ice cream (which / that) I bought.
- We went to the village (which / that) Lily recommended.
- John met a woman (who / that) I had been to school with.
- The police arrested a man (who / that) Ram worked with.

(Clause after the subject)

- The bike (which / that) I loved was stolen.
- The university (which / that) she likes is famous.
- The woman (who / that) my brother loves is from Mexico.
- The doctor (who / that) my grandmother liked lives in New York.

Non-defining relative clauses:

We don't use 'that' in non-defining relative clauses, so we need to use 'which' if the pronoun refers to a thing, and 'who' if it refers to a person. We can't drop the relative pronoun in this kind of clause, even if the relative pronoun is the subject of the clause.

(Clause comes after the subject)

- My student, who is very nice, lives in Manchester.

- My sister, who I live with, knows a lot about bikes.
- My bicycle, which I've had for more than eleven years, is falling apart.
- My mother's house, which I grew up in, is very small.

(Clause comes after the object)

- Yesterday I called our friend Ram, who lives in Agra.
- The photographer called to the Queen, who looked annoyed.
- Last week I bought a new dress, which I don't like now.

Exercise

Join the following pair of sentences using defining relative clause.

1. The music is good. Julie listens to the music.
2. My brother met a woman. I used to work with the woman.
3. The country is very hot. He went to the country.
4. The job is well paid. She applied for the job.
5. The dog is over there. The dog's / its owner lives next door.
6. I live in a city. I study in the city.
7. I sent a gift to my sister. My sister lives in America.
8. I ate the mango. I bought the mango.
9. My friend lives in Australia. My friend is a doctor.
10. The woman was arrested. I reported the woman to the police.
11. Imran is good- looking. He's Sherlin's brother.
12. Dublin is the capital of Ireland. It is my favorite city.
13. My brother is an Engineer. He can speak 5 languages.
14. My friend is 22. He comes from Dubai.
15. London is the capital of England. It is one of the largest cities in the world.
16. Tom has starred a lot of films. He is a famous American actor.
17. My school is very big. It is in Rameshwaram.
18. The new band plays music. Rajesh works there.
19. My sister is 20 years old. She spent her holiday in ooty.

20. I met Mr.Sachin at the trade fair. He is a famous cricketer.
21. We visited St. Mary's Church yesterday. It is very old.
22. Can you find the teacher? You talked to her this morning.
23. Mary is a very charming girl. Her brother is a friend of mine.
24. I wrote a letter to my mother. I forget to post it.
25. Kamatchi is having a child. She lives three flats away from us.

Answers:

1. The music (which / that) Julie listens **to** is good.
2. My brother met a woman (who / that) I used to work **with**
3. The country (which / that) he went **to** is very hot.
4. The job (which / that) she applied **for** is well paid.
5. The dog **whose** owner lives next door is over there.
6. I live in the city **where** I study.
7. I sent a gift to my sister **who** lives in America.
8. I ate the mango **which/that** I bought.
9. My friend **who/that** is a doctor lives in Australia.
10. The woman **who/that** I reported to the police was arrested.
11. Imran, **who** is Sherlin's brother, is good- looking.
12. Dublin, **which** is the capital of Ireland, is my favorite city.
13. My brother, **who** is a teacher, can speak five languages.
14. My friend, **who** is 22, comes from Dubai.
15. London, **which** is the capital of England, is one of the largest cities in the world.
16. Tom Cruise, **who** has starred a lot of films, is a famous American actor.
17. My school, **which** is in Rameshwaram, is very big.
18. The new band, **where** Rajesh works, plays great music.
19. My sister, **who** is 20 years old, spent her holiday in ooty.
20. Mr Sachin, **whom** I met at the trade fair, is a famous cricketer.
21. St. Mary's Church, **which** we visited yesterday, is very old.
22. Can you find the teacher **whom** you talked to her this morning?
23. Mary, **whose** brother is a friend of mine, is a very charming girl.
24. I wrote a letter to my mother, **which** I forget to post.

25. Kamatchi, **who** lives three flats away from us, is having a child.

Idioms

An idiom is a collection of words in common usage that have a meaning that cannot be deduced from the meanings of the individual terms. For example, rain cats and dogs (meaning “rain very heavily”) are an idiom; and over the moon ("extremely happy") is another idiom.

Idiom Meaning

A blessing in disguise a good thing that seemed bad at first

A dime a dozen Something common

Beat around the bush Avoid saying what you mean, usually because it is uncomfortable

Better late than never Better to arrive late than not to come at all

Bite the bullet To get something over with because it is inevitable

Break a leg Good luck

Call it a day Stop working on something

Cut somebody some slack Don’t be so critical

Cutting corners Doing something poorly in order to save time or money

Easy does it Slow down

Get out of hand Get out of control

Get something out of your system Do the thing you’ve been wanting to do so you can move on

Get your act together Work better or leave

Give someone the benefit of the doubt Trust what someone says

Go back to the drawing board Start over

Hang in there Don't give up

Hit the sack Go to sleep

It's not rocket science It's not complicated

Let someone off the hook To not hold someone responsible for something

Make a long story short Tell something briefly

Miss the boat It's too late

No pain, no gain You have to work for what you want

On the ball Doing a good job

Pull someone's leg To joke with someone

Pull yourself together Calm down

So far so good Things are going well so far

Speak of the devil The person we were just talking about showed up!

That's the last straw My patience has run out

The best of both worlds An ideal situation

Time flies when you're having fun You don't notice how long something lasts when it's fun

To get bent out of shape To get upset

To make matters worse Make a problem worse

Under the weather Sick

We'll cross that bridge when we come to it Let's not talk about that problem right now

Wrap your head around something Understand something complicated

You can say that again That's true, I agree

Your guess is as good as mine I have no idea

Exercise:

I.Complete the sentence with Idioms:

1. Ramesh failed his examination but his mother came and said just one thing, "Son, __________
2. I ____________ against him for not taking me into confidence.
3. Walter made the dance team _______________, you see the audition gates were about to get closed.
4. My cat is _______________ after playing the whole day.
5. He is absolutely terrified of skydiving, but he thinks once in my life, he will ___________
6. Ram felt like a ___________when his girlfriend took him to a Zoo.
7. She was willing to __________ for the love of her life, Mithun.
8. Juli better ____________ if she wants to make big in foot ball.
9. She was murdered in _________
10. When grandfather saw her grandson collecting coins like her son used to do, he knew he was a ____________

I. **II. Each of the following idioms followed by four meanings. Find out the correct one.**

1.Curl one's lip

a. show scornb.grinder c. show score

2. To a hair

a. vaguely b.exactly c. get away

3. Face the music

a. listen to the music b.get reprimanded c.give up

4. To take heart

a. to become hopeful b. to put off c. personal

5. To draw the line

a. to decide b. to set limits c. to suspect

III. **The idiom/italicized in the sentence is bolded in the following questions, and four choices are given. Choose the option that most accurately expresses the meaning of the provided idiom/idioms.**

1. Her arrogant behavior with friends has left her **high and dry**.

a.To be penniless b. To be very sick.

c.To be very famou d. Isolated

2. I had to **break the bank** to but these bags!

a. Things will get better b. To be very expensive

c. Face the reality d.Show score

3. Maria told **a big fish story**. It is not even necessary to listen!

a. Person who failb. person got success

c. unknown d. exactly

4. Ramu and seenu finally saw **eye to eye** on the business deal

a. agree b. disagree

c.depressed d. Cheerful

5. **He's kicked the bucket**

a. Studying b. Good luck

c. died d. throw

6. I realized that you don't like the shirt he sent, but, it is a gift, so please, **don't look a gift horse in the mouth**.

a.don't judge it by price b.don't compare it with others gift

c.don't find fault with the gift d.don't expect too much

7.The surprise quiz came **out of nowhere**.

a. be quiet b. to tell the secret

c. unexpected d. timepass

8. My loud friends need to **put a sock in it**.

a. be quiet b. very easy

c. trick someone d.bad situation

9. Johnson is not very excited, he is **laid back.**

a. last chance b. relaxed

c. to leave d.to contact

10. I can't go to the beach today; I have to **hit the books.**

a. help someone b. calm down

c. unexpected d. to study

Answers:

1. Don't cry over spilt milk.
2. Bear a grudge
3. By the skin of his teeth,
4. Down for the count
5. Give it a whirl.
6. Fish out of water
7. Go the extra mile
8. Step up her game
9. Cold blood.
10. Chip off the old block.

II.Each of the following idioms followed by four meanings. Find out the correct one.

1.a. show scorn

2.b.exactly

3. b. get reprimanded

4. a. to become hopeful

5. b. to set limits

III. The idiom/italicized in the sentence is bolded in the following questions, and four choices are given. Choose the option that most accurately expresses the meaning of the provided idiom/idioms.

1. d. Isolated

2. b. To be very expensive

3. a. Person who fail

4. a. agree

5. c. died

6. c.don’t find fault with the gift

7.c. unexpected

8.a. be quiet

9. b. relaxed

10. d. to study

www.ingramcontent.com/pod-product-compliance
Ingram Content Group UK Ltd.
Pitfield, Milton Keynes, MK11 3LW, UK
UKHW022024190726
13853UKWH00005B/2093